NEWSLETTER NINJA

TAMMI LABRECQUE

ISBN 978-0-9982127-5-3

v. 190416

www.newsletterninja.net

Contents

For my students.
You've got this. Keep killing it out there.

Foreword - by David Gaughran

I'VE BEEN self-publishing for seven years. That's quite a long period to be screwing up almost the entire time, but I managed it! My whole approach to email was backwards. I did all the don'ts, ignored all the warnings, missed out on so many opportunities to build myself a happy and engaged audience of readers that it causes me literal pain when I think about it. I don't say this to elicit sympathy. Rather, I hope that my long experience of doing exactly the wrong things can act as a deterrent—a giant sign made of bones spelling out "Here Be Wolves."

What did I do exactly? I only emailed people when I had a new release. I thought I was being considerate and not clogging up everyone's inboxes when, in reality, I was only turning up at their door when I wanted something: their money. This was compounded by my slow production speed, particularly with those painstakingly researched historical novels I seem to enjoy writing for some reason. That problem was further exacerbated by working in more than one genre, so the books came out even slower and the emails were even less frequent. Clearly, I felt I wasn't antagonizing my most loyal readers enough with this set-up, so I decided to have one Frankenlist—my fiction and non-fiction peeps all lumped together—neatly ensuring that everyone really wouldn't care about at least 50% of the (increasingly infrequent) messages I was sending out.

Yeah, I was officially Bad At Email.

There were more insidious effects too. Deep down I knew I was Bad At Email, but instead of this manifesting in some change of tack, I retreated into myself. Messages became less personal. I lacked confidence—dreading launch day instead of getting a thrill of anticipation when hitting my list. Because I knew I'd see a continuation of several disturbing trends: falling opens, reduced clicks, less conversions, increasingly tepid engagement, and then people unsubscribing or marking the email as spam as the final kick in the teeth. How did I get here? And how did I climb out of that hole?

I started listening to Tammi, is the short version. She started teaching a course on email and I was one of the first people to sign up. Yes, I was at least partly motivated by wanting to support a friend, but Tammi sounded like she knew her stuff and I was beginning to accept that I needed to radically change my approach. I had already taken one important step: I had separated those fiction and non-fiction readers. But I didn't really know what to do next, and I was hoping I'd get some ideas from Tammi's course.

Eh, yeah.

Within a month I had started a brand-new mailing list with a five-part automated onboarding sequence, during which I doled out my custom-written reader magnet which was getting rave reviews. I had pivoted to a weekly newsletter approach and weeded out the dead weight on my old list, and open and click rates were climbing.

Within two months I had launched my first book to these new readers, and it hung out at the top of the charts for a considerable time. My newsletter subscribers were responding in greater numbers than ever because my "ask" (and a new release is still an "ask" because you are looking for their money!) came after a string of "gives" for a change.

Within six months I had re-energized my existing non-fiction list and had a brand-new list containing thousands of new readers— passionate and engaged and loyal subscribers who not only opened and clicked but actually looked forward to getting my emails. I know this because they email me and tell me! I can't explain to you what this means to me, how much I have been reinvigorated by this. My whole career feels like it has been rebooted, and I look to the future with confidence rather than trepidation. I get a tingle again every time I hit my list.

I don't know where you are in your career or whether you have made all these mistakes too. If you are just at the beginning of your journey, you have the chance here to do things right from the start. But if you have screwed things up as badly as me, I want to give you the confidence that you can turn things around—remarkably quickly too. Even quicker if you haven't ticked every box on the Giant List O'Mistakes!

So, just listen to Tammi, learn how to put value in every single email, and start building a passionate list of engaged readers. I wish I did it years ago.

Acknowledgements

ACKNOWLEDGEMENTS ARE *HARD*, y'all. But here goes:

I would be an ingrate and a fool not to make a special point of thanking David Gaughran—for his wonderful foreword, his insistence that I must write this book, and his many glowing recommendations of the course that gave birth to it. But most of all, I have to thank him for his unfailing friendship. It's by no means a certainty that when you meet your heroes, they will be every bit as wonderful as you've imagined. I got lucky.

Chris Fox has been my dear friend for several years now, and I have literally no idea what my life would be like without him. He was the first person who believed in my ability to be an editor, the first person who told me I could be a teacher, the first person who convinced me that the things I knew had actual real value to my fellow indie authors. His faith in me is the bedrock on which

I've built every good thing over the last 3+ years. There aren't words enough to thank him.

The members of Authors' Corner have done so much for me, and become a special sort of family. I love you guys so much.

My IPI students make me smile every day, and I'm so proud of all their accomplishments, big and small. Whether it's a good launch, a high open rate, or an ass-kicking ad, every time they succeed, I feel like part of me succeeds as well.

Sean Platt championed this book with his usual enthusiasm—which is a great deal of enthusiasm indeed—and the rest of the Stone Table buoyed me with their approval and excitement.

Sondra Turnbull, Christine Mancuso, Mike Omer, and Michelle Hart read pieces of this manuscript hot off the keyboard, gave me encouragement and redirection, and cheerleaded (cheer-led?) me ever onward when I wanted to give up. It may be true that only I could have written this book, but I couldn't have written it without them.

And, lastly, while I was building my author and publishing business(es), my daughters Isabella and Caroline didn't see me for longer periods than I care to admit, put up with a lot of penny-pinching, and ate a great deal of takeout without complaining (though perhaps that last part wasn't so bad). You two are my heart and soul, and the best things that have ever happened to me.

1 - Who Am I (And Who Are You)?

THE FIRST PART of that question is easy (for me, anyway). My name is Tammi Labrecque, and I'm an indie author, editor, and publisher. I write and publish my own books under a couple of pen names, and freelance in what feels like every related field, from plot doctoring to editing to ads management. I've been writing since I was a tween, was traditionally published in the olden days (the 90s), and I've been doing this indie publishing thing since 2014. You might have seen me on the Self-Publishing Podcast, met me at the Smarter Artist Summit or 20 Books to 50K Vegas, worked with me when I was employed at Sterling & Stone, or heard about me from clients like Chris Fox, Wayne Stinnett, or David Gaughran.

I've done just about every job there is in the indie publishing space, but—apart from writing—newsletters are my favorite thing. They're *my jam*, as the kids say. (I have no idea if the kids still say that, or if they ever did, but let's not go down that rabbit hole just now.)

Now for the second part: Who are you?

We can assume you're an author, or maybe an author assistant. Either way, you've got an email issue. Generally, people come to me with one of three problems:

- They want to start a list but aren't sure where to begin, or
- They've got a list but it's not as big as they would like, or
- They've got a list that's big enough, but not engaged.

No matter which of those statements applies to you— or even if you're a hybrid of those things, or stuck somewhere between two of them—I can help. I maintain my own mailing lists as well as several lists for other authors, I helped with the vast email enterprise that is Sterling & Stone, and I've been running month-long sessions of a class called Mailing List Expert (MLE) for almost a year now, testing out these techniques with students across the entire gamut of genres, mailing list sizes, and approaches. The stuff I teach *works*—and, more than that, it will make talking to your list fun instead of a chore you have to check off around release day.

Let me pause for just a moment and make one thing clear: I am definitely not going to walk you step-by-step through the actual button-pushing of creating a list, making a signup form, or what queries to run to tell who's opening emails or how many unsubscribes you got or anything like that. There are *dozens* of email marketing providers (Mailchimp, Active Campaign, and the like), and it wouldn't be remotely practical of me to try to cover all the technical steps required to get each of them up and running—to say nothing of ongoing maintenance. So you will have to work through that part yourself.

If that's daunting, there are resources to help you. Many virtual assistants will handle email for you. Author friends can give you tips. The email marketing services themselves have help and support documents, and varying levels of customer service to help you answer your unique questions about your own circumstance. I, and many other people, offer classes or consultation that can address your individual situation. But if you were looking for a book that would deal in those kinds of specifics, you should definitely return this book. That's not the value proposition here, and I have a near-phobia about not delivering value.

This book is intended to be about a mailing list *philosophy*, a new way for you to approach the problem of email and make it easier and more fun for both you and your subscribers. This book will give you the foundation to seek out those more specific answers, because you'll know what questions to ask. And yes, we will talk about every step of the process, but always in terms of how to approach the topic, ways you might do things differently, things you might not have thought of, pitfalls to avoid, and fun stuff like that.

But we have a couple of things to address before we get to any of the fun stuff.

Now, before you nod off—or skip to something that looks more interesting—know that this technique is one you'll be using a lot, to great effect, when it's time to start your new approach to your email list, so you might as well learn it. It's called *answering the reader's objections*.

"Wait a minute!" you're probably saying. (If not, you can go ahead and say it now, if only to make me feel better.) "How can I have any objections? We haven't even begun."

Okay, that's a fair point. But the thing about answering objections is that it's ten times more powerful if you answer them *before they even arise*. So let me answer yours, even though you might not have developed them yet or known you had them.

I've been teaching a class on this for a while now, and I've seen the objections that arise as students go through mindset shifts and learn new techniques and all that groovy stuff. Apart from the most common objection, which is something along the lines of "But I don't *want* to write an onboarding sequence," most people's objections generally fall into two camps:

- I would never subscribe to (or stay on) a list like the one you're describing, and
- I'm just an indie author; people aren't interested in what I have to say.

If you don't actually have either of those objections,

bear with me while I treat them as a rhetorical device. If you *do* feel that way, though, and you've been letting those thoughts stand in the way of your newsletter success, get ready—because I'm about to tell you that both of those statements are bollocks. Let's turn the page and talk about why.

2 - You Are Not Your Reader, But You Are a Rock Star

You Are Not Your Reader

IT HAPPENS every time I run a class, and in every consulting session I do about email. It happens when I'm just sitting around with my indie author pals and put forth some tenet of newsletter philosophy I believe in (we indie authors are a real blast to hang out with, as you see). I'll suggest something that seems pretty tame to me, something like "Email monthly" or "include cat pictures," and someone is sure to say "That would turn me off," or "that would make me unsubscribe," or "No way would that work on me."

Well, good for you, you newsletter-hating edgelord. And what have you got against cats?

My response to this is something I say to students so often that I'm thinking I might get a tattoo, or at the very least have a rubber stamp made: Do not make business decisions based on your own consumer behavior.

One more time, for you clowns in the back throwing pencils and passing notes:

Do not make business decisions based on your own consumer behavior.

This is a huge mistake, and I see so many people make it.

So what do you do instead? You make decisions based on how your readers respond to things you try—by getting reader feedback and by looking at measurable results (open rates, click rates, unsubscribe rates, conversion), not by guessing or defaulting to behavior that accommodates your own biases.

Because there's good news, and the good news is this: *You are not your reader*. I cannot stress that enough. Even if you read widely in your genre, even if you subscribe to author newsletters, you are not your reader. You are an author, and you view author newsletters through your own prism. Things that are intolerable to you as a consumer are not necessarily intolerable to your readers— and, in fact, may be things your readers like!

All those things that turn you off, that would make you mash the unsubscribe button? I'll give you ten to one, the majority of the reader audience you're trying to tempt onto (or keep on) your mailing list simply *loves* those things. And I can prove it to you—but, even better, you can prove it to yourself. Because everything I will tell you to do is something you can test and split-test and test again, letting your own list tell you what they do and don't like. (*Split-testing*, what some people call A/B testing, is the process of offering consumers two different things and tracking which gets a better response. We'll talk about it more a bit later.)

And all you have to do to make this work is to be open —open to trying new things, open to the idea that not everyone shares your disdain for autoresponders or polls or cover reveals or cats, open to the possibility of finally having the mailing list you want/need/deserve/whatever. All you have to do is make a pact with yourself that you will be guided by actual metrics instead of feelings.

Easy-peasy.

But You Are a Rock Star

My response to the second objection—*I'm just an indie author; no one cares what I have to say*—is something along the lines of "Baloney" (mainly because I already used "bollocks"). You are not *just* an indie author. To the people who have read your book or downloaded your reader magnet (we'll talk in depth about reader magnets later; for now, just know that they are a thing) or found you in whatever manner they found you, and then signed up to hear more from you, *you are a rock star*. (I won't repeat myself this time. I trust the pencil-throwers were able to maintain their attention span for a few paragraphs.)

How can you be a rock star when you're just ... well, frankly, just *you*? That's easy: because to the reader, you're not just *you*. You're someone who wrote a book they loved enough to hand over their email address—a commodity that is getting more and more precious as our email inboxes become fuller and fuller—so they could learn more about you. That's real, and it's powerful. They *like* you. They are already predisposed to be interested in what you have to say.

So I won't repeat it, but I encourage you to repeat it to yourself from time to time—maybe when you're casting about in vain for something to write about in your next email, and thinking that you might just skip sending one this month, as you've nothing to say and who wants to hear from you anyway? Say it: "I am a rock star."

Then say it again, and mean it.

Does that sound like some kind of *woo-woo*? Like perhaps I've read *The Secret* one (or ten) too many times? It won't, if you stick with me through the whole process.

So if you're ready to embrace your inner rock star and be your reader instead of yourself for a while, let's start at the very beginning: Why do you need a mailing list?

3 - Why You Need a Mailing List

YOU NEED A MAILING LIST. I don't suppose I have to tell you this, as you've just forked over money that could have been spent on a pint, or some doughnuts, or admission to a movie—granted, at one of those theaters with the sticky floors and wobbly cup-holders, but still. You could be watching the next installment of *The Fast and the Furious* instead of hanging around listening to me bang on about mailing lists, so I'll try not to waste your time.

But just in case we have any holdouts in the "I don't need a mailing list" camp, bear with me while I run through the rationale.

Yes, you need a list. A list that lives in a database that you can access at will, whose signup forms you control, with fields and parameters and specs that you set. A list that belongs to *you*, which is the thing that separates it from your super-cool reader group on Facebook, or the subreddit you hang out in, or your two hundred (or two hundred thousand) Twitter followers.

If you're thinking, "Thank you, Captain Obvious, defender of all things already known," I feel you, my friend. That's some 101 shit, right there. We all know you need a damn list. Every indie publishing "guru" has been flogging this particular deceased equine for lo these many years now.

Nevertheless, there are still people out there—and I do not get these people *at all*—who will resist building a mailing list, or, if they do build one, will resist using it to its full potential. They have fallen into the trap of believing one or more myths:

- A list is too much work.
- I can get by with Facebook/Twitter/Instagram/my website.
- People can follow me on Amazon/Bookbub/Draft2Digital.
- No one does email anymore anyway.

In order:

- No, it's not.
- No, you can't.
- Yes, they can, but then you don't know who they are.
- Yes, they do.

Don't get me wrong—using the other platforms is

great. There are people on each of those platforms for whom that is their preferred method of connecting. Those are all ways you can talk to or at least have a presence for your people. I myself use many of them.

But building your business on somebody else's platform is a terrible idea. If the primary place where you interact with your reader belongs to someone else, you're doing something that I've heard called *digital sharecropping*—toiling on someone else's land to produce something, to their ultimate benefit rather than your own. Sure, you might get a subsistence living out of it, but you're never going to own anything worth talking about if you just keep bringing your readers over to someone else's platform.

Your list is *yours*, and (if you treat them right, which we will get to) can be leveraged swiftly and effectively when you need something. The importance of that can't be overstated.

Let me give you a recent and painful personal example. I'd already taught this class four times—and told upwards of 40 students that they needed to understand those other platforms could disappear in the blink of an eye—before I experienced it for myself. And it was pretty terrible.

In one of my other lives, I'm a romance author. As such, I love Facebook. My readers, by and large, are already there, and they're forming communities and swapping book recommendations and cheerleading for their favorite authors night and day. It's really quite beautiful. I had an amazing reader group of just over

1800 people, but because I didn't want to have to do all the upkeep myself, I had built the group with another author; we built it together and were both Administrators. We were BFFs, so what could be more fun than me and my good friend hanging out with our readers, talking about books (and ogling hot guys, because romance readers are some of the most sex-positive and totally shameless people on this planet, for real)? It was, without question, the best, most fun, most responsive reader group on Facebook.

And then my friend and I had what I thought was a minor disagreement, and she removed me from the group with no warning. I had to start over.

Now, all the mailing lists in the world aren't going to ease the sadness of losing a good friend—but if you'll allow me to compartmentalize, what I want to talk about here is what I did to start that new reader group. I think you know what's coming: I turned to my mailing list. In just a few days, I had hundreds of people in the new group. It was a far cry from 1800, but that 1800 didn't happen overnight, so I knew that was fine. It would grow. (It would grow a lot faster if I published more books than I do, but alas.)

What's important to note is that if I hadn't had my mailing list, the new group would have been comprised of me and however many readers saw my Facebook post about it. And if you've tried to get some visibility on a Facebook post lately, you know how hopeless that would have been. The mailing list saved the day.

Another excellent argument for a mailing list over

social media is that email converts better than social media. (For the purposes of this discussion, "convert" is, basically, a reader doing the thing that your email/post/what-have-you is encouraging them to do— buy, click, reply, choose, whatever.)

Why does email convert better than other avenues? There are some definite measurable reasons: more people use email than Facebook (though Facebook is catching up!), they check their emails first and more often, and they just prefer to be sold to in email rather than Facebook. (I'm using Facebook here because it's the most popular social media platform; the others lag behind it quite a bit in terms of use and conversion.)

But, based on what I've seen and what I know about how people use the internet, I think I can add a couple of more nebulous theories.

First, there's a certain level of buy-in that comes with someone giving you their email address. We all get too much email, so handing out your email address is not as simple a choice as it used to be. People's inboxes are already too full, so choosing to let you in there means that their interest in you is high. When you send an email, they should be primed to respond positively—by opening and clicking. If you give them something irresistible to read and/or click on (more on how to do that later), you have an almost guaranteed buy-in from them. That's really powerful.

Second, there's a lot less distraction in email. If you make an offer to someone on Facebook, it's competing with so many other things. If you make an offer in email, the reader is focused on you—at least for the length of time it takes to read that email. There's a whole different flavor to their reception of what you are saying when they open an email vs. seeing you in their Facebook feed, surrounded by cat videos and baby pictures and ads—if they even see you in their feed, which is frankly getting harder and harder all the time. Without all the distractions, you've got an opportunity—possibly a brief one, but an opportunity—to speak directly to your reader while you have her full attention. And that is also really powerful.

Whatever the reasons, everyone agrees: email converts better. One good analysis can be found at http://bit.ly/EmailVsSMed.

So now that we're all on the same page, and agree that one must have a mailing list and afford it pride of place in one's stable of reader interaction techniques, let's talk about what a mailing list really is: who it's for, what it's for, and some important guidelines for how to use it to its greatest potential.

4 - My Mailing List Philosophy

THERE ARE a fair number of people making a living in the "advice to authors" segment of the indie publishing space. A smaller but still not insignificant number of them either specialize in email/newsletters or at least devote a portion of their business to teaching about them.

So what makes me different? Basically, I think it comes down to my core philosophy, which can be generally summed up in two parts:

- **First**, you are not selling what you think you are.
- **Second**, if all you're using your list for is selling, you're doing everything wrong.

That's it, my whole mailing list philosophy in two sentences. But since you paid actual money for this book, and since those two sentences are a little vague, let me expand on them. I'm going to do it in reverse order, because while I think I've listed them in order of importance, they actually build on each other the opposite way.

If all you're using your list for is selling, you're doing everything wrong.

Most people who come to me with underperforming mailing lists mean the same thing when they say "underperforming": People are not opening, not clicking, and/or not converting to buyers. The author sends out emails like clockwork asking people to buy books, and then *if* people open them (which many do not), they're not buying. If you think the purpose of your list is to sell books, this can be incredibly frustrating. But I'm going to argue that if you're deciding on the worth of your mailing list by looking at sales and conversions, you're measuring the wrong thing. If you send an email and your only expectation is "They should click the link and buy the thing," you're not doing email right.

Why? Because *you are not selling what you think you are.*

Every student who comes to me—every single one, so far, without exception—thinks they're selling books. They finish the class with a very different perspective, one that can be hard to convince them of, but that ultimately ends with satisfied writers *and* readers. The primary purpose of your newsletter is not to sell books (though if you do things properly that will be a happy side effect). The primary purpose of your newsletter is—or should be—to build what David Gaughran calls "superfans": people who don't just love a book you wrote, but also love *you*, and subsequently love *all* the books you write.

When you invite people to your newsletter, and send them emails, you aren't selling books. *You are selling yourself.*

This is quite a paradigm shift, but if you can wrap your head around it, it makes all the difference. It makes perfect sense, if you think about it. After all, *yourself* is the only thing you've got that no one else does. Amazon is awash with books—flooded to the point that we're all drowning, readers and authors alike—so it's not like readers have subscribed to your list because it's the only way they can find a book to read. No, they're there because they liked *your* book—and, it naturally follows, since you wrote the thing, they like *you*. No one else can give them that.

So, yes, in the world at large, you are in the business of selling books, but on your email list you are in the business of communicating with your readers and building relationships.

When you come to understand that the people on your list are there not just because they want to know when you have a book out, but because they want to know more about *you*—as an author, as a person—you approach your list in an entirely different way. You can be more relaxed, more open (within your own comfort zone), more free to be your authentic self. And this new, more genuine approach will cement fans to you even more, changing them from interested readers to superfans who will go out and evangelize for you with other readers, helping to build the little (or maybe big) reader army with which you will conquer the world (or at least the bestseller charts)!

But to get there, you have to internalize what I've said above, and you must come to understand that a lack of responsiveness in your mailing list is not a subscriber problem—it's a *you* problem. Most people with underperforming mailing lists are simply not handling them right. That's a tough pill to swallow, but the good news is, now that I've told you that, I'm going to tell you how to fix it.

First, though, we're going to run through some really basic software and setup stuff, just to make sure the novices know what to do and the veterans are using best practices. Sounds fun, right?

(I'm just gonna pretend you said yes.)

Onward, then!

5 - Planning and Setup

THE FIRST QUESTION most people ask me is, as you might expect: *Which email marketing service should I choose?* And it's not a bad question—all of the various services have pros and cons; they do different things, at different price points, with different levels of flexibility; and what's right for you might not be right for someone else—but I think it's the wrong question with which to begin.

The proper first question, I contend, is: What do you need your mailing list to be able to do?

If you start there, rather than with price or gimmicks or what the author you want to be like uses—if you decide what you need from your email marketing service (which I'll be calling an EMS from now on, because I'm lazy and don't want to type it out every time), *then* choose the service that's right for your needs —you'll be in a much better position to leverage the one you choose, because you will have chosen it for reasons that make it specifically suited to the list you're trying to build.

Choosing an EMS

So how do you go about deciding what you want your list to be? If you already have a list, a good place to start is with your current situation. Which things are working, and which are not? From there, you can extrapolate what a good list (for you, because this is quite individual) would look like.

If you don't yet have a list, or much of one, it can be a bit hypothetical in nature—though I contend it's still helpful to ask yourself the questions.

Are you wide (selling in all stores rather than being exclusive to Amazon)? Are you cross-genre? Fiction and/or nonfiction? Do you have pen names? Do you have overlap between pen names and genres?

The answers to these questions allow you to decide what level of flexibility you need with regard to segmentation, separate lists, tagging, and things of that nature. If all that sounds like so much gobbledegook, don't worry; we'll talk about all those things a bit further along. For now, just be aware that if you write in more than one genre, or write both fiction and non-fiction, or have two pen names with no overlap at all, you may be fine with an EMS that places people on separate lists and does not allow you to send an email to more than one list at a time (at the time of this writing, MailChimp and AWeber are like this).

If, however, you anticipate that a substantial number of subscribers would wind up on more than one list, or if you want to be able to send (or not send) an email to specific subsections of a larger list, you would probably be better off with an EMS that allows you to combine lists and tagging (or custom fields) to send emails in a more targeted or more inclusive manner, whichever is right for your circumstance. Otherwise, you'll find it quite inconvenient to send an email to those overlapping subscribers *and* you may be charged twice for them each month when it comes time to pay for the number of subscribers on your list(s).

How often do you grow your list using things like newsletter signup swaps, cross-promotion bundles, giveaways, etc?

Non-organic or incentivized subscribers need to be onboarded in a different way than organic subscribers (again, we'll get to those concepts in just a bit), so you'll have the same need for segmentation or tagging or some other way to know who came in from where, which will allow you to send them down different paths when they join, and to isolate them later if you need to send them something specific or engage them in some particular way.

How big is your list?

This affects price, obviously, with MailChimp and Mailerlite having fairly robust free options (up to 2,000 and 1,000 subscribers, respectively, at the time of this writing), and others starting at more expensive price points but becoming more equitable as subscriber numbers rise.

How often will you send emails?

Some services have a limit on how many emails can be sent in one month, which may or may not depend on your specific plan; you should definitely read the fine print to make sure you're not locking yourself into a list that can't expand without costing a lot of money.

If you are an infrequent sender, a less expensive plan might work well for you, or you might like MailChimp's plan that charges per email rather than per month. I don't really address this sort of plan or approach, because you aren't going to be an infrequent sender once I'm done with you.

How willing are you to move your list from one EMS to another?

Moving is not as hard as some folks make it out to be, but it's not a whole lot of fun either—and I would argue that you have better things to do. Additionally, with recent changes to privacy laws in the EU, and the near-certainty that changes like those will find their way across the pond, it's worth mentioning that moving lists will involve a lot of tracking signup information to comply with any subscriber requests for information. And who needs that hassle?

However, if money is an issue right now, but you anticipate needing more advanced features down the road, it's definitely possible to start on one of the free or less-expensive services and move later. I generally advise beginning as you mean to go on, and starting out with the best choice for the author business you envision; I also understand that sometimes that's not possible.

What is your budget?

I like to ask the budget question *after* the other questions, because starting with budget immediately eliminates some services from your list of possibles. Better instead to evaluate all the services before determining your budget, for two reasons. One, you will have a better idea of what's a fair price for each level/type of feature; and two, you might decide that a certain EMS's features are desirable enough that you're willing to budget a bit more than you might otherwise have done.

Now that we've answered all those pesky questions, we're ready to choose an email marketing service.

The Best EMS

I get asked the same question by just about everyone at or near the beginning of class: *Which EMS is the best one?* I hope you'll forgive me for side-stepping the question, but it's impossible to say which is the best EMS—only which is the best EMS *for you*. I can usually come up with a pretty good answer for any individual student, because we talk about their specific situation, but I can't give a definitive answer that would apply to everyone reading this book.

For one thing, this is one of those "it depends" situations, and I can't give a recommendation for each possible combination of answers to the questions above. For another, I want this book to be evergreen, so to speak —still useful in a few years, or even longer—and things change all the time in this business. Even advice that's really solid today may not be so tomorrow—and will certainly not be so in two years.

So, in lieu of a recommendation for you personally, I will say this: Take stock of all the questions I asked above and then research every EMS you can find, paying special attention to any that come highly recommended from your peers. The top dogs, at the time of this writing, roughly in order of ease-of-use, features, and expense, are: Mailerlite, MailChimp, ConvertKit, Active Campaign, AWeber, and Drip. But ask around; by the time you're reading this, the landscape could have changed drastically.

And, as I said above, to whatever extent is possible for you, make price point your final deciding factor rather than your first. Do your best to afford the EMS that best fits your needs, if you can—and if you can't, make finding that money in your budget a top priority. This is worth doing right.

While we're on the topic of software: If you're going to offer some sort of reward (what I call a *cookie* or *bribe*, and normal people usually call a *reader magnet*; we will talk about these at length later) for joining your list, you also need to consider how you're going to deliver that reward. Some mailing list services will allow you to include attachments to welcome emails or emails in an automation sequence (we'll get to those topics soon!), or you can always include a link to a file stored in a cloud-based service or on your website. I have done those things, and they work, but the tradeoff is that you will inevitably wind up doing customer service for people who can't figure out how to download, side-load, open, or otherwise partake of your brilliant reader magnet due to difficulties with technology.

As I said just a moment ago, I want this book to continue to be useful long after it's published, so I'm hesitant to recommend any specific tactical advice, preferring to focus on strategic principles. (We'll talk about the difference between tactics and strategies in a later chapter.) So rather than endorse any particular way of accomplishing this reader magnet delivery, I'll just say that you should look around (and ask friends) for a solution that allows you to offload delivery and customer service to someone else—for example, some sort of service that would *funnel* your *books* onto a reader's device.

(*Stage whisper: I'm talking about BookFunnel.*)

Initial Setup

So once you've done all this planning and choosing, you just have to set up the structure of your list(s) and get them ready for the subscribers you don't have yet. Setting up your mailing list is fairly simple no matter what EMS you end up choosing, but as with so many other things, you will make it easiest on yourself with some advance planning. Every EMS is different, so it's not practical for me to attempt to explain the step-by-step process for each of them. If you don't know how to create a list or make a signup form, your EMS will have customer service documents (or possibly chat or email) that you can consult to figure out the basics.

The questions you asked when you were determining which EMS is best for you (cross-genre? overlapping subscribers? lots of list-building?) will be useful again here, as you set up your lists, segments, tags, custom fields, etc.

And, as I've said, if you choose one service and then find out down the road that it's not flexible enough for your needs, you can always switch. Try to start as you mean to go on, but it's better to start a list when it's 80 percent "right" than to wait until it's perfect—because it's never going to be perfect.

So get yourself up and running with the best practices you can manage and the best service you can afford, and don't be so afraid you'll do something wrong that you do nothing at all.

That said, once you think you've got everything set

up the way you want it, take your own email address through the signup process to make sure everything looks and works as it should. There may be things you need to change to make the process seamless and professional-looking.

To use an example from my own experience, when I sent out the first ActiveCampaign email for one of my romance pen names, the name in the *From* field was my own. This was not a huge tragedy, because that pen name isn't a big secret, but it was confusing for subscribers who had signed up to Nom de Plume's email list but got an email from a name that many of them didn't recognize. It was time well spent digging around in the settings to figure out why that was happening and how to fix it.

In fact, you'll want to test *everything* on yourself before deploying it. Signing up, automated emails, regular campaigns, unsubscribing—anything that a subscriber might do or see, you should do or see it first. Again, this is worth doing right. It looks unprofessional when emails don't have the right name on them, or placeholder language is accidentally left in, or an image is pixelated, or whatever (the list of things that can go wrong really does seem infinite sometimes, but you must just do the best you can), and why look unprofessional if you can help it?

Believe me, you'll do plenty of looking unprofessional over the life of your list. For example, you might, I don't know, participate in a list-building cross-promotion, set up a beautiful onboarding sequence for those new subscribers, then import them with the wrong tag and send them a confusing email that leads to a bunch of unsubscribes. If you do, I recommend doing it just before the release of your book on how to be a Newsletter Ninja, because what could be more fun or less embarrassing?

Now that we've done our planning, we need to get some people in here, right? Nope, still no. There's a reason I've placed the chapters of this book that deal with list-building *after* things like setting up your list, creating an onboarding sequence (I keep using that phrase, and I promise we'll get to it next chapter), and figuring out who (and where) your perfect subscribers are: Because you don't want people flooding—or even trickling—into a list that's not ready for them. So before we start acquiring subscribers, we must first plan, then set up (then do a couple of other things, actually, but we'll talk about that in just a minute).

In short: we've got a few things to do yet. And we're going to do them in a weird backwards order for a little while, setting up the onboarding sequence, then the welcome email that precedes it, and lastly the signup process. Why? Because you don't want a list signup that goes nowhere; you need the signup to lead to the welcome email, and then into the onboarding.

So let's get this thing ready for subscribers, *then* we'll talk about who those subscribers are and how to attract them.

6 - Onboarding

Onboarding Basics

OKAY, so we're finally here—the mythical onboarding sequence! So what exactly is an onboarding sequence? It's the autoresponder that introduces people to you and convinces them to stay on your mailing list.

Let's back up just one step and define the word *autoresponder*, because that's obviously important. An autoresponder, in general, is an automated email that is triggered to send when a subscriber takes a certain action. Unlike what we normally think of as a newsletter, which is written at or near the time you will send it and talks about current events—a book you're working on now, a sale you have coming up soon, when your next release will be, etc—an autoresponder is something you will write only once, and is meant to be fairly "set it and forget it." You can have an autoresponder set up for when a person clicks a certain link, or has been on the list for a specific amount of time, or has a birthday, or whatever you like.

Or—and this is where it gets cool—when someone first signs up, you can have an autoresponder that gives them an overview of your work and makes them think it would be fun to stick around for more of your emails; this is an *onboarding sequence*. (You're bringing the subscribers "on board," so to speak.) It begins when your autoresponder is triggered by people joining or being added to your mailing list, and goes on for however long it takes to accomplish the two goals I just stated.

Your onboarding sequence can consist of as many or as few emails as you like. I have a romance pen name whose onboarding was a single email for quite a long time, because she only had two books and a single email was more than enough to introduce her to readers. As you develop more things to talk about—and a deeper backlist —your onboarding sequence may get longer, and that's fine, too. But it should never be so long that you're struggling to find something to say.

Actually, this is advice that you would do well to apply to *all* emails to your list, automated or otherwise, but it's especially important here. This is the all-important "getting to know you" phase for you and your subscribers, and they don't yet love you enough to be forgiving of unnecessary—or worse, *boring*—emails.

That last bit—the bit about how subscribers are just getting to know you—is important. Generally speaking, people who are just joining your mailing list will have had, at best, a few intersections with you—maybe they've read a book or two; or seen you at a Facebook takeover; or joined during a list-building promotion, so they have your reader magnet downloaded but might not even have read it. While it's true that the focus of this book is building a mailing list full of people that love you and everything you do, you should never abuse that by sending emails that don't matter—and this goes double for your onboarding, where you can be fairly certain that a new subscriber knows little to nothing about you.

But they will soon! The onboarding sequence is where you fix that—where you not only introduce yourself, but begin the essential task of showing these people how awesome you are.

The Purpose of Your Onboarding Sequence

So, your onboarding sequence has a few jobs to do. It needs to introduce new subscribers to you and your work, prepare them for the experience of being on your mailing list, and leave them wanting more. In fact, *each* email in the sequence should do at least two and hopefully three of these things.

How you do that is really up to you; as with a few other mailing list topics, it's virtually impossible for me to offer specific advice, because a successful author newsletter is unique to the author who created it and the people who receive it. I can offer a few guidelines, though.

- Make your sequence as long as it has to be to

give a good overview of your work, and no longer.

- Offer something personal in each email—a funny anecdote, a peek behind the scenes of writing a specific book, a picture of your cat— within your comfort zone, of course.

- Make sure the first email reminds them how they ended up on your list. This, more than almost anything else you can do, will greatly decrease the number of unsubscribes you get in those first few emails, and will almost entirely eliminate Spam reports, which you (obviously) do not want.

- End the sequence by telling them what happens next ("You'll hear from me about once a month" or "You'll receive my biweekly newsletter and release notifications"), thanking them for letting you introduce yourself over the course of the last few emails, and inviting them to interact with you somewhere else, too, if there's somewhere you hang out more regularly (a Facebook group, a subreddit, a genre forum, etc). While I truly believe the newsletter is king for building your fanbase, there's something very powerful about the kind of quick, everyday chatting that happens in more interactive places—especially places where fans can talk not just to you but to *each other*. Let them build or join a community that includes you or is centered around you, and they'll identify strongly with it.

- Somewhere in the sequence, give them something of actual value besides the cookie (which you'll recall from last chapter is the signup reward for people who join your list). I like to do this toward the beginning for organic subscribers but toward the end for non-organic subscribers, because non-organic subscribers need to be discouraged from sticking around in hopes of free stuff—more on that in just a moment. This can be something free from you, something free from someone else (perhaps a link to a book you know is permanently free), or even just a really good bargain (your first-in-series that is always 99 cents, for example).

I tend to offer freebies to organic subscribers, because they already like me and will be quality subscribers from the beginning, and offer bargains to non-organic subscribers, because this helps to weed out the people who only want free books. Those people can clutter up your list for ages, and you're paying for them not to open your emails, or to open them and never click on anything that might cost them money. I hope I've made my point that your list is not *just* a tool to sell books, but you're not running a charity here, either. If someone never, ever clicks on anything other than a free book, they should be first in line when it's time to purge the dead weight (which we will talk about at the end of this book).

All that said, keep in mind that not all non-organic subscribers are the same. You'll hear from a lot of people that building any kind of list other than a completely organic one is a terrible idea; I think that's hogwash. Some list-building promotions will net you pretty high-quality subscribers, others will get you thousands of people who don't give a single damn about you and never will. We'll talk about this some more in the Straight-Up Bribes chapter.

All *that* said, it is true that, in general, your organic subscribers are going to be high-quality from the start, and they should be treated very well. Again, we'll get to more detail on that; just file it away for now.

If you follow those guidelines, tweaking them to your specific genre(s), subscriber avatar(s), and personal disclosure comfort level, you'll have a series of emails that intrigues as it informs, and makes subscribers look forward to your next email.

Designing the Onboarding Sequence

So, great, that's what your sequence should *do*. Now for the big question: How do you set it up? There are almost as many answers to that question as there are people to ask it, so let me once again just give some general pointers.

Your onboarding starts right where your signup form leaves off—and that means if you have different signup forms in different places, you need to decide whether everyone goes through the same onboarding, or if you create a custom onboarding sequence for all the places where you might be picking up subscribers, or something in between.

Some authors like to keep it extremely simple. Maybe every subscriber who joins their list, regardless of where they signed up, goes through the same series of onboarding emails and ends up on a single list, to which the author can then send his regular campaign emails.

Other authors get really granular about this, setting up different signup forms for each possible subscriber source (we'll discuss this more in the list-building chapter); delivering a different reader magnet to each subscriber based on where they signed up; building a separate onboarding sequence for each of those signups; and/or creating separate lists, tags, or custom fields, so that any individual group or type of subscriber can be isolated and interacted with in a situation-specific way.

As an aside, let me make a suggestion. If you do want to have a different cookie and/or first onboarding email for each subscriber source, that's awesome (in fact, I encourage it), but do yourself a favor: Write them in such a way that each can lead into the *same* second email in the sequence. If your onboarding will have four emails, only write emails 2-4 once, and write those initial emails to flow naturally into a single single email (and subsequent emails) that will go to everyone. Then your onboarding sequence looks like a beautiful tree, with many branches all feeding into one main trunk, and you've saved yourself from writing three additional emails for every new subscriber source. I'll elaborate on this just a bit in the next chapter.

I have helped many authors set up sequences like this, and they're actually a great deal of fun, but they require a lot of maintenance. Most authors I know who have a really elaborate onboarding have a virtual assistant to help out, because it takes a great deal of time and requires a skillset that doesn't always come naturally to an author. I get a lot of requests to build and maintain this kind of setup, and while I'm always happy to build, it's very rare for me to agree to ongoing maintenance, because it's *very* time-intensive. This is the main reason I suggest that people rein themselves in as much as they can while still achieving their goals.

But the authors who keep it super simple or go hog-wild are, in my experience, in the minority. Many authors, including me, wind up somewhere in the middle. For expedience, I'll use myself as an example again:

I break down my subscribers into just two categories. There are "organic" subscribers, who sign up at the links or forms found on my website, Twitter, and Facebook, go through a three-email onboarding sequence, and then drop onto my main list. Then there are "giveaway" subscribers, who go through a different, four-email sequence, and then if (and only if) they have opened every email, automatically move over to my main list. (If they open some emails but not others, there's a small extra automated loop to make sure they want to be there —and that I want them!—but that's my own personal quirk.) As I detailed above, each giveaway subscriber receives a first email that reminds them how they got on my list and delivers the cookie for that source (plus picks up a tag that tells me where they came from). But then each of those emails ends with the same promise about when I'll send the next email and what will be in it, and from that point on everyone gets the same series of three more emails. It works beautifully, and is considerably less work than creating an entire unique sequence for everyone.

Your organic subscribers—the ones who sign up from your back matter or your Facebook page, or some other location that they found after reading one of your books—are generally a higher quality of subscriber than ones you get through less organic methods. These are readers who sought you out and signed up because, one can assume, they liked what you wrote and would like to see more of it. We love these readers, and we onboard them and treat them differently.

Some people never mingle their organic people with their incentivized people, and that's an absolutely valid way to do things. I have a compelling reason to do it the way I do: I'm lazy and a bit scatterbrained. If I have to create slightly different content for different types of subscribers, and then remember to send that content to multiple lists, it just makes me less likely to do the most important part, which is to communicate regularly with all of my subscribers. So once someone makes it through my onboarding, which I think is pretty rigorous and weeds out the people who aren't likely to be enthusiastic subscribers, I throw them on the main list and call it good. You may choose to do something different, and of course that's fine. As I've said, each author is unique, and so should their newsletter be.

So, once you've decided on the basic flowchart of where people will come from, what tags or custom fields they might acquire, and what path they will follow until they ultimately exit your onboarding sequence, all you have to do is actually write the onboarding emails. *So great, right?*

Well, not really! You've got things to do and every five hundred words of email you write for your onboarding sequence is five hundred words you didn't write in your current work-in-progress. But this is important, so let's figure out how to make it as easy as we can on you.

7 - The First Date

WHEN I'M TEACHING MLE students, I frequently compare their onboarding sequences to the dating process. It sounds silly, but it's also a decent comparison, if I do say so myself. In these initial emails, you are introducing yourself to your new subscribers, and you're also watching their actions and responses to see if they're a good fit for you.

And, as with dating, many won't be. As we've discussed (ad nauseam, really), that's fine. Enough of them will be a good fit that you can build up quite a stable of ... dates? (I guess this is where the dating analogy breaks down—unless we want to get into polyamory, which is really outside the scope of this book. *Ahem.*) So the key is to write these initial emails in a way that highlights all your best qualities while at the same time sending subtle signals to those who aren't right for you that they can show themselves out.

However, before we get to the brilliant emails you're

going to write, there's a little bit of automated business over which you only have partial control. If you have your signup set to require double opt-in (which you should, without exception), your email service provider will send out both a confirmation email and a welcome email. It's not a bad idea to take a look at those and optimize them as best you can.

The Confirmation Email

First up is the confirmation email. When someone puts their email address (and whatever else you ask for; we'll get to that in the next chapter) into the signup form and submits it, they will get a message that they need to confirm their email address. So off they go to their email inbox to find the confirmation email. Our hope is that it's sitting right there at the top of the inbox ready for them to click-to-confirm and get this party started.

Sometimes, however, it won't be. Even here, right at the beginning, that email may go to a Spam folder (or, in Gmail, possibly the Promotions tab). Savvy subscribers will know to look for it there, but—and this is important— not everyone is a savvy subscriber. Without intervention from you, there is a non-zero percentage of subscribers who won't see the email, will shrug and figure "Maybe it will come in a little while," and move on to do something else. *This person may never see that email.* They might forget about it, or try to sign up again and give up when the email still doesn't come.

Help those nice people out. When they click to

submit their information and sign up, they will see a message on the signup page, or will be redirected to another page (this will vary, depending on your service and your setup). Make sure that the first thing they see after hitting *Submit* is instructions on how to do two things: First, how to check their Spam folder and Promotions tab and pull your email out of them; second, how to whitelist your email address so that your future emails will not be diverted out of their main inbox.

Whitelisting is the process of letting an email provider know that emails from a specific contact are trusted emails, and should never be sent to Spam or Promotions. Some email providers require that the receiver add the address to Contacts, or an address book, or what-have-you. There are actually quite a few ways to do it, depending on the email provider. In the Helpful Links section, I've included links to several different pages that explain how to whitelist; you should make one of these available to your subscribers.

When should you give them these instructions? Well, I include whitelisting instructions in literally every email I send; it's that important. But nowhere is it more important, or more likely to be successful, than in this first contact. There is no better time to get someone to whitelist you than when they have just fished your email —an email they know they requested, and therefore might be peeved about not receiving—out of somewhere other than their main inbox. A subscriber who just had to go hunting for your email is going to be more receptive to instructions about how to prevent that from happening.

So definitely include whitelisting instructions everywhere a subscriber's eyes might land in the signup process and the confirmation email.

I also recommend adding a header graphic or some other image that aligns with your branding. My romance pen name has a very specific website design, and the header graphic in her emails carries over that branding, using the same fonts and logo. Right from this first confirmation email, I'm starting to build my brand in the subscriber's mind.

The Welcome Email

The second email that subscribers will receive is generally another automated email, this one welcoming them to the list or thanking them for subscribing or confirming. Depending on your EMS, it may simply tell them their subscription was successful. Some services also include signup information like what IP address was detected during the process, or password information, or any manner of things.

The important thing from our perspective is that, like the confirmation email, this is almost always something that you can customize. And as with the confirmation email, I recommend branding and whitelisting instructions.

But there's one pitfall to avoid here: Many authors put a link to their cookie in this welcome email. Do not do this, because in doing it you miss a key opportunity to increase the deliverability of your newsletter.

We'll talk about deliverability at length when we get to that chapter, but for now I'll just touch on one aspect of it. The automated welcome email may have your email address in the *From* or *Reply-To* field (which is great), but the subscriber's email provider can see that it came from a Mailchimp server, and quite possibly not the same one that will handle your ongoing emails. Without getting into the technical mumbo-jumbo (which, to be perfectly frank, has been explained to me a dozen times and still doesn't quite click), basically, there's a decent chance that Gmail or whoever won't see this email as coming from *you* the way it will see your automations or regular newsletter.

Why does this matter? Because every time an email from you is delivered to a subscriber, the email providers are watching to see what the subscriber does with that email. Does she open it right away? Does she click on the links inside? Does she reply to it? Those actions contribute to your sender reputation (which, again, we'll discuss when we get to the chapter on Engagement), and it behooves you to begin building your reputation as early as possible. If the email in question—the one the subscriber does a lot of interacting with—comes from MailChimp instead of you, you won't get the "credit" toward your sender reputation.

So use the welcome email to thank the subscriber for confirming, and to direct them to find a new email from you—an email which contains their cookie. Nothing works so well to get someone looking for an email as telling them there's something cool inside it for them!

Your Onboarding Sequence Begins

That email that they go looking for is what we will consider the first email in your onboarding sequence, and you can do pretty much whatever you want with it (and what you want, incidentally, is to entice people to open it, give them something cool to click on, and solicit a reply).

When they open that email, it should of course be tightly branded like everything has been up to this point, and it should definitely contain whitelisting instructions, though you can include them at the end instead of beating people over the head with them. This will be the third time you've talked to them about whitelisting in the last quarter of an hour, and they may well be tired of hearing it, so feel free to dial it back a notch.

In addition to your tight branding and your incessant banging on about whitelisting, you want two things in this email: the link to your cookie and a question for them to answer.

The link to the cookie is easy, and you're pretty much guaranteed a click; this is, after all, probably the reason they signed up. Composing a question they'll feel compelled to answer is harder, but not impossible. We'll talk about what makes a good question when we get to the Engagement chapter, because it's worth doing right. As I keep saying, every interaction a subscriber has with your email(s)—opening, clicking, replying—contributes to your reputation; this is a golden opportunity to get the trifecta. And in your first real email, no less! Gmail is going to looove you. (Not really, but they might be slightly less hostile, and we take what we can get.)

But all this preceding business can be summed up neatly like so: these first few emails are an opportunity to talk to readers when they first sign up, and it should not be wasted. Welcome them, offer whitelisting instructions, give cookies, build up that history, and start training them.

You have to start fighting right from the start to make them understand that if they want to see your emails, they probably have to do something proactive. And many of them won't do it, or won't do all of it, but you will continue to show them what they have to do throughout the sequence.

Okay, so now that we've got confirmation, welcome, and cookie delivery out of the way, what next?

Well, first, give them a damn break. They just ran an exhausting gauntlet of subscribing, hunting up emails, clicking on cookies, and (one hopes) whitelisting you. Wait a couple of days before you send anything else.

When you send your next email, make it short and sweet—a check-in to see if they got the cookie is the standard, and it's really the perfect thing to do, so why reinvent the wheel? If you're doing your own cookie delivery, you'll end up getting some replies to this email that will require customer service from you—explaining to people how to get the cookie onto their various devices, mostly. If you've contracted this out, you can just direct subscribers how to access customer service for whoever is doing your cookie delivery.

One more domino down; they're all confirmed and welcomed and full of cookies (yum). Now what?

Now—finally!—you get to show them a little of the ol' razzle-dazzle. (Do yourself a favor, and Google "razzle-dazzle meme." Endlessly entertaining.)

Your Onboarding Sequence Continues

So, with the preliminaries out of the way, let's look at the onboarding sequence proper, which I recommend you start 7 days after initial signup, and 5 days after the check-in email. You can do it sooner (though not much) or later (though not so late they forget you), but 7 days is a good workable span of time.

This email they get after the check-in is the prime time for you to introduce yourself and your work. Tell them who you are (again), remind them how they ended up on your list (yes, again), and link to your cookie (yes, *again*). Then give them a little background on you—your favorite books growing up, maybe, and what you write, and a few personal details if you're comfortable with that. Remember, it doesn't have to be your bank PIN; even "I love tacos and *The Bachelor*" qualifies as personal detail— and if in fact you do love those things, the people who also love them will begin to identify with you. And the people who don't will, one hopes, forgive you for your terrible taste in TV shows. (Everyone loves tacos, so that part shouldn't cause any problems.)

This is a good point to mention that you very well might want to tailor that email to take into account where a subscriber came from. For example, if they signed up organically, you might greet them differently than if they came through a paid list-building promo. If you're the sort who has more than one cookie, each initial email will deliver the cookie you've designated for that particular signup source, and subsequent emails might deliver other cookies in a specific order, as you gradually work your way through the genres or series that best relate to that cookie. As we talked about in the previous chapter, there are almost as many ways to set this up as there are authors.

Follow-up emails should follow a natural arc. First, introduce yourself and talk about some aspect of your work, or one of the genres you write in, or your first book, or your favorite book. Use subsequent emails to explore other genres or parts of your catalog, or tell them what you love about certain books you've written, or explain how your series relate to each other. Do what works for you, based on your books, but make sure every email leads naturally into the next and that the sequence tells an overall story. You're an author. You can do this.

But don't feel like you have to write a long or elaborate sequence. Remember: as long as it needs to be, and *no longer*. And make things as multi-purpose as you can, so that you're not duplicating effort where you could conserve that creativity for, you know, writing your books.

I am, as I said, lazy and scatterbrained, so I keep it as simple as I can. You might recall that I divide my subscribers into just two categories, organic and giveaway. I have a short onboarding sequence for organic subscribers, because people who seek out my website to sign up have almost certainly read at least one of my books and are already predisposed to like me. The tone and number of those emails is therefore a bit different.

I have another onboarding sequence for subscribers who come to me through non-organic means—giveaways, cross-promotions, etc—but just one. I *could* set up a separate onboarding sequence for all the possible entry points, but there are a *lot* of non-organic ways to get subscribers. If I set up a separate onboarding for (just throwing out examples here) every Bookfunnel cross-promo, BookSweeps list-building giveaway, or newsletter swap, I would be recreating the wheel many times over, with only subtle changes.

What I do instead is exactly what I recommended earlier: I tailor the first email in the sequence for each new subscriber source, while attempting to only have to write one version of subsequent emails. So my first email might say something like "Hi, thank you for downloading my novella in the January 2018 Bookfunnel Romance Bundle!" or "You're here because you entered to win a free book at Booksweeps"—that sort of thing. With this method, everyone in my "giveaway" onboarding sequence gets a relevant first email to introduce me, personalized to acknowledge how they got on my list. Then *the next three emails are exactly the same.* In a flowchart, Emails #2-4 would be lined up one right underneath the other—nothing fancy, but with any number of Email #1s pointing to a shared Email #2. This will save you a ton of work and hassle; as I mentioned in the last chapter, you only have to write those subsequent emails once, and there's nothing I love more than working once and benefiting in perpetuity.

When I add a new source, like the Bookfunnel bundle I'll be doing later this month, I just duplicate an existing Email #1, change up the relevant details, and voila—new introductory email, but I do a minimal amount of work to tailor that email, and I never have to rewrite or even duplicate the rest of the sequence.

And, of course, in each email in the sequence, I aim for a killer subject line (more on that later), at least one awesome thing for subscribers to click on, and a question they'll really want to answer. Remember the triad: open, click, reply. Get them to do at least one of those things every time you send them an email, and by the time they make it to your main list or start getting your regular campaigns, you'll be several lengths out in front of the authors who don't have your exceptional email game.

This, like everything else we've discussed, is worth doing right, but don't make it so convoluted or difficult that you won't want to set it up or maintain it; even a good onboarding sequence should be evaluated a few times a year, and subsequently updated or revamped to include any changes in your catalog or availability or what-have-you. So don't have fifty onboarding sequences that you have to completely rewrite every time there's a change. Save all that effort for writing books—that is, after all, what your subscribers are waiting for!

8 - The Sign-Up Process

OKAY! Now that you've got everything set up for subscribers (and tested it yourself, don't forget!), let's do a quick overview of signup forms—but first let's talk for a minute about what it really *means* for someone to sign up for your list.

We've already talked about this from the subscriber's end—it means they love you and they're fortunate to be able to receive your weekly or monthly brilliance in newsletter form. Obviously.

But you also need to think about what the signup requires from *you*. Yes, having someone sign up for your list is awesome; it means they like you, and (one hopes) will find your newsletters both edifying and entertaining, and (one *really* hopes) will launch your new books into the top 5 on Amazon (and you into that pied-à-terre in Paris, or whatever your particular dream is). But you must always remember that your newsletter signup is a contract between you and the subscriber. They gave you an email address, and you've promised them some things in return (or you will have, once you've got things set up properly).

- You told them they'd get something for signing up—a free story, maybe, or some cool swag, or just a periodic update on you. (We'll talk more about this later.)
- You told them you'd never share or sell their email address. *Don't.* I'm not even going to try to crack a joke about this, because it's absolutely serious. Never betray the trust your subscribers gave you. Just don't. For one, it's a lousy thing to do. For another, it's illegal. (Some folks will tell you that, *technically*, you can't sell email addresses but you can "rent" them. Personally, I tend to avoid people who make moral or business decisions based on what they can *technically* get away with. I urge you to do the same.)
- You told them how often you'd email them and why. This sets expectations, and it also might send them looking for an email if they're expecting one in two days and it doesn't come.
- You told them, or at least implied, that your newsletter will entertain or inform them, and it should always do so. As I said before, do not send unnecessary or boring emails. Respect your subscribers' time—and your own!

Those are just a few things you might have promised; there are more. Things about you, about the list, about the goodies, about myriad things. But what's important here is that whatever you tell them at signup, you have to stick to it and be consistent.

This is another reason you have to make decisions before starting, because once you've said "I'll send you a free story," you're obligated to make sure that you get that free story to them in a timely and convenient (for them) fashion. Once you've said "I'm only gonna email you when I have a new release" (please don't say that!), you're stuck.

If you want to change up an ongoing promise you made, you have to give your subscribers a chance to *nope* out of it. You have to email them and tell them what the changes are going to be, and give them a chance to unsubscribe if that's not what they want. And you'll lose folks, every time.

But if you do the signup process properly in the first place, they'll know what to expect. The key is that while you're enticing them with your brilliant mailing list bribe, you also need to make sure your signup is clear about what you plan to do once you have their email address. To wit: "We are gonna have some conversations; this is not just a place where you'll get a free book and then you'll never hear from me, or where you just get an email every two days about somebody else's book on sale, or whatever. That's not how this will be." (I'm paraphrasing. Obviously you say it better than that, and probably not quite so bluntly. Say it like yourself—your *authentic* self!)

Be clear about what they're getting, and they won't sign up if they don't want it.

Do You Want All the Subscribers?

Hold up a second. I hear you freaking out, because I've just said (*super* casually), "Then they won't sign up"—am I freaking crazy? You want them *all* to sign up. You want every person to join your email list, so they'll buy your awesome books, right?

No.

You don't want all the people; you want the *right* people. The ones who are there for the one thing no one else can provide—which, as we've discussed, is *you*—not the ones who are just there for the next book fix. Those people are maybe not the exact right people for you. You don't need them.

I know I sound cavalier when I say "Whatever to them, we don't need 'em," but we don't need 'em. You are building a list—a strong list—of people who like you, like what you have to offer, and will become advocates for you. That's the kind of fan that you want, the kind of person who pushes your books into someone else's hands and says "You've got to read this, this author's so cool."

So if folks sign up because you've got a little reward (which is perfectly fine), they can take the reward and run, or they can stay and get to know you a little bit better. If they're the right subscribers for you, they'll want to stay; if not, they'll hit the unsubscribe button.

And if they *do* unsubscribe, now or in the future?

That's fine as well. Make sure your goodbye email (or the unsubscribe page they land on, or whatever final communication you have with them) says something like, "If you just want to know when I have a new book, follow me on Amazon or follow me on Bookbub" (and give them links to do so). Some authors even maintain a separate list for people who only want release emails. I don't do this—frankly, Amazon and Bookbub have way better deliverability than I do—but it's a valid option.

But whichever option you choose, just try to catch them as they unsubscribe, in a way that will allow them to still buy things from you but not be in that dedicated fanbase you're building. Because you are truly building a fanbase, not a bunch of people who may or may not open, and may or may not buy. Remember that. Believe it. There are plenty more subscribers where those came from, and you will gradually pull in more and more of them, letting the disinterested ones fall by the wayside, always building up that core of true superfans.

Your Signup Form(s)

So now that we've gone through what it means for someone to sign up, and why they should (or shouldn't) let's talk about the actual mechanics for a minute—the signup form itself.

The one field that every signup form must have (literally; there is no mailing list service that would even allow you to create a form without it) is, obviously, the

Email Address field. This is, after all, how you'll send the newsletter. Wow, ground-breaking stuff, huh?

But apart from that, you have some options, and we should talk briefly about those. Most services allow you to ask for a wide array of standard information—first and/or last names, dates of birth, gender, age, birthday, phone number—and, if you use custom fields, virtually anything else you might want to ask. None of it is strictly necessary, and much of it is off-putting to a new subscriber.

Rule of thumb: Every item of personal information you ask for will lose you a certain percentage of potential subscribers. Once they've turned over their email address, many subscribers will begin to eye with suspicion any further questions from you. "Why does she need my last name?" they'll ask, or "I'm not sure I want to give her even my first name." And, for *sure*, "What the hell is she going to do with my phone number?"

So, sure, you can ask them their birthday because you want the software to send them an automated birthday greeting every year … but it might be better to wait until they've been through your onboarding, and then give them the *option* to update their information to include their birthday if they want to participate in that.

Personally, I ask for a first name, but I don't make it a required field. Having a first name makes it possible to have the subscriber's name show up in the subject line or in the email itself, which personalizes it and increases open rates. But you have to pay attention to whether the subject line or sentence where the subscriber's name appears is going to sound ridiculous or nonsensical without the name. If it is, you must either require it of everyone (which, again, will lose subscribers before they even sign up), compose your emails in such a way that they still make sense with the name missing, or resign yourself to weird emails with sentences like: "[First Name], I've got big news for you!" or " , my new book is finally here!" This is, needless to say, not terribly professional.

To Tag or Not to Tag—and How

One final thing you can do with signup forms is use them to tag or segment subscribers as they join—either behind the scenes or right out in the open. I'm a fan of behind-the-scenes, but let's touch on both.

Some authors like to have visible checkboxes or some other way for subscribers to segment or tag *themselves* as they join. A signup form like this might ask readers to choose which retailer they purchase on, or whether they want to receive all your emails, or only emails about a particular genre or even a particular series. And, of course, the dreaded "Check this box if you only want to hear about new releases."

Some providers allow for forms that do this; some don't. If yours doesn't, I wouldn't sweat it. I don't really like to let new people self-segment anyway, for a couple of reasons.

First, at that point readers don't know you yet. They don't know what they're going to get from you, nor do they know how awesome you are. So they might choose "New releases only" when your monthly campaigns are a *blast* and they would become one of your superfans if only they had the chance to read a few of them.

Second, if you're looking at tagging them by something like genre or interest, they'll either choose the option that they hope will result in fewer emails, or they'll choose everything and defeat the purpose of tagging them in the first place. (I believe most self-tagging should happen during regular campaign emails, and we'll talk about that in the chapter on delivering value.)

You may want to do some behind-the-scenes tagging of your own, however. When someone uses the form on my website to join my list, my EMS tags them as "organic." That's a segment I want to keep my eye on, always. They are almost without exception the first to open, the most likely to click, and the most responsive to questions. My open rates for that specific segment of the list are reliably 80-85%, which is spectacular. (Open rates on the list as a whole are not nearly so good.) If I need to deploy those loyal subscribers strategically, I want to be able to parse them out of the surrounding noise with ease.

As far as what tagging or segmenting options you should build into a signup form, that's another one of those "it depends" situations, and the options are too varied to get into in a general book like this. One word of advice I *will* give, as it's pretty universal, is this: tag/segment *way more than you think you'll need to.* I'm embarrassed to admit how many times I've sent a campaign or built an automation, only to decide later that

I wish I'd set a link to tag who clicked on it or set up an automation to tag someone or move them to a different list. I end up going behind myself, building segments after the fact, and that's not a good use of my time—not when I could have handled it on the front end, at the planning stage.

As with many things involved here, begin as you mean to go on, and you'll have set up the perfect list—or as close as you're going to get without sending some actual people through this whole process.

That means, we're ready—finally!—for subscribers. Now we just have to figure out who they are and go find them.

9 - Your Perfect Subscriber

YOUR MAILING LIST, I am fond of telling students, is a bunch of little points of light that all need nurturing. And despite not normally being the kind of person who says things like "people are little points of light," I truly believe this.

That said, though, you can't talk to a thousand people, or ten thousand people, at once. I mean, you can, but it's not going to resonate the way speaking to each reader individually will.

"Wait, what? Speak to each reader individually? I've got shit to do, Tammi!"

I know. That's why we'll shortcut our way to that ideal one-on-one dialogue, by creating a subscriber avatar to stand in for those little points of light. This allows you to send emails that resonate with all your subscribers—every one of them a unique individual who shares at least (and maybe only) one thing: a love of your writing—without driving yourself mad trying to tailor your emails to however-many thousands of people.

Creating subscriber avatars is one of the first things we do in *Mailing List Expert.*, and it's the thing people seem most skeptical about. (It's not the thing they *least* want to do—that distinction is reserved for writing autoresponders—but it's up there on the list.) Admittedly, the process is a little strange, and at first it feels very unnatural, but I believe it's crucial to mailing list success.

So what is a subscriber avatar, and how do you create one?

Reader Avatars vs Subscriber Avatars

Subscriber avatars are similar to reader avatars, but with some key differences. Before we talk about them in depth, let's talk briefly about why we want to differentiate them.

First, you need to come to grips with one very important truth: *Not everyone who might like your books will necessarily like your newsletter*. This can be hard to reconcile with our desire to have every single person who might ever buy a book from us join our list. The author with the biggest mailing list wins, right?

Well, not necessarily; in fact, almost certainly not. The author with the most *engaged* mailing list wins—and, generally speaking, a smaller list will be more engaged, though the cause-and-effect actually goes in the opposite direction. A list is not engaged because it is smaller; rather, the process of building an engaged list means that those readers who are only somewhat interested in you will not stay subscribed to your newsletter (and that's *totally fine*, as we discussed in the previous chapter), and those that stay will be your biggest fans.

The first step to creating this list of superfans is figuring out who your perfect subscriber is. While your perfect reader is not necessarily also your perfect subscriber, reader avatars are a great place to start, because your readers and your potential subscribers do share at least one similarity: they like your books. That might actually be the only thing that you can say with certainty is true of all of them, but it's a pretty important one, no?

But even though your readers have that in common, when it comes to joining your mailing list, they diverge. *Not all your readers will be good subscribers.* (Add this to the list of tattoos I'm going to get, I guess.)

So let's talk about how are they different, and why it matters.

A reader avatar is by its very nature a broad portrait. Something like: "My readers are age 35-60, upper- to middle-class, have white-collar jobs, enjoy fast-paced books, and read mostly on the weekends." When you are trying to sell books, you have a more generic reader avatar because you want to sell those books to as wide a swath of people as possible. (Or, rather, you want to sell them to the widest swath of people who also read books like yours. The *why* of this is way outside the scope of this discussion, but has been covered in detail by many people who explain it better than I do. Two great resources to start understanding it are Chris Fox's book *Six Figure Author* (you can buy that at amzn.to/2OPqAL3), or *Amazon Decoded*, a short book that you can acquire by signing up for David Gaughran's newsletter at DavidGaughran.com.)

But a subscriber avatar is not a broad portrait, and for very good reason. We create broad *reader* avatars because we want our books to appeal to many; we create focused *subscriber* avatars because we can more easily talk to one person at a time. Your mailing list will be made up of many people (hopefully many, *many* people), but it's daunting to talk to thousands of people in a way that feels naturally intimate. So when you compose an email campaign for your subscribers, it's often helpful to imagine that you're writing to one specific subscriber.

It's an interesting line to walk; you want to address the email to your wonderful readers (plural), but when you're actually writing the content, it will naturally be more interesting and relatable if you are speaking to one person. At some point, you may come to know some of your subscribers well enough that you set your subscriber avatar aside in favor of actual subscribers who've responded to you (and this is a wonderful situation to find oneself in). But when you're starting, do yourself a favor and create a subscriber or two that you can address in your emails. You'll avoid the stiff nature of emails designed to appeal to everyone (which somehow always end up appealing to no one), and you'll find it much easier to be your authentic self.

So your subscriber avatar, then, becomes *very*

specific. She's not 35-60; she's 38, married, with one kid and another on the way (and, apparently, a woman). She's not middle-class with a white-collar job; she's a financial manager with a health-care conglomerate, and she and her husband (a teacher) make enough money to afford a good day care and a very nice house in Austin, Texas. Hell, give her a backyard pool, too; it's hot in Austin. She loves James Patterson, though she really only has time to read for a half-hour or so before bed, and on Saturday mornings when her husband takes their kid to soccer practice. Give her a name. This one's Pamela.

Now, when you send a newsletter, aren't you going to have an easier time relating to Pamela (who might even be a lot like you)? Won't you naturally write your emails to appeal to someone like her, and in so doing write a friendlier, more enjoyable and relatable email?

I contend, quite fervently, that you will. And if you disagree, don't tell me—because it works amazingly well for me, and for my students and clients. If we've only been succeeding by fooling ourselves ... well, I don't want to break the spell.

Now, will you alienate everyone who is not a 38-year-old financial manager? Of course not. Some things are universal: the joy of being a parent (stop laughing), the frustrations of a high-pressure job, trying to find time for self-care when our lives are so busy, navigating a marriage or relationship, worrying about money (even if you make quite a bit), daydreaming about a tryst with Chris Hemsworth or Scarlett Johansson (or both!). Having an avatar to think about when you're composing an email allows you, almost paradoxically, to address specific universal themes that you would miss if you were trying to talk to however-many thousands of people, none of whom is exactly like the next.

And, interestingly, by speaking to a specific person, you reveal more about yourself than you otherwise might. Because we're very different when we're sharing one-on-one than when we feel put on the spot to be open with a great big bunch of strangers. Obviously, some people are more open than others, and you shouldn't feel pressured to reveal anything more than you're comfortable with. But remember that being personal can be something small—a movie you loved or a picture of a pet. People *love* pictures of pets, and will respond with pictures of theirs. Like, always.

The cool part is that these subscriber avatars will, in a way, become a kind of self-fulfilling prophecy. When you address your emails to your subscriber avatars, you will naturally attract people who are like those avatars. It's not easy, and it's not necessarily fast, but boy is it effective.

So now that we know what our perfect subscribers are like, we're almost ready to go find some. But first we need to do one final thing: we need to chat briefly about the difference between *strategies* and *tactics*.

10 - Strategies vs Tactics

WAY back in the Planning and Setup chapter, I told you we'd talk about the difference between strategies and tactics. This is the perfect time to address that topic, because before we dive into methods of list-building, we need to understand that there are many tactics for building your list—but they change frequently, and you can only stay on top of the current tactics by understanding the strategy behind them.

So what's the difference? In brief: *Strategies* are general plans of action to achieve a goal. *Tactics* are the individual things you do to implement that strategy.

Seems simple enough, but it's *incredibly* important— both to your success with your newsletter, and to your success as an indie author in general. Understanding of this concept is a big part of why some folks are successful and some are not, even if they seem to be doing the exact same things. If you look closely, it often turns out that the successful author did something—let's say he started using a new advertiser that catered specifically to his genre—then a lot of other authors began to do it, too, and it stopped working as well. At that point, our hypothetical successful author saw that the industry had changed, and that he'd have to do something new to accomplish what he wanted, since the old thing isn't effective any more. So perhaps he seeks out some social media channel or Internet forum where readers of his genre tend to hang out, and figures out a way to become part of that community and sell without overtly selling. (This works, by the way, and again I have to recommend *Six Figure Author* if you'd like to expand on ideas like that.)

He can no longer implement his old tactics and achieve the same results. His *strategy* (finding new readers in his genre) hasn't changed, but his *tactics* have—and the people using the old tactics are left wondering why this thing that seemed to work so well actually doesn't, while our savvy author is prepared to pivot at any time and find new tactics to remain successful.

Let me elaborate with an example that every indie author understands:

Having a funnel starter (what many businesses call a "loss leader")—is a *strategy*. A loss leader gives a consumer a free or discounted taste of what you have to offer, to tempt them into wanting more at full price (or to tempt them into buying something else in the store, or accessories, or what-have you), and virtually everyone who sells *anything* does this. This is a time-honored strategy that will probably persist until people stop trying to sell things (so, forever). But the most effective *tactics*—what you use as a loss leader, for example, or how you call attention to it or deliver it—will almost certainly change over time.

Currently, making the first book in your series permafree on all the ebook retailers is a *tactic* that helps you accomplish your goal of getting people into your funnel (unless your other books are enrolled in Kindle Unlimited, but again, that's beyond the scope of this book). Other tactics might be: creating a sampler of short stories in your story world, using that as a cookie, and driving traffic to it with Facebook ads; or setting up a newsletter swap with another author in your genre (you send your list a link to their cookie or another book, and they do the same for you); or setting up a bundle on Bookfunnel where many authors offer their cookie or a free book, and then all the participating authors drive traffic to the bundle page. You can employ a variety of tactics to implement your strategy.

I'll reiterate, because it's very important: *tactics change*; strategies, by and large, don't. So what works to get people into your funnel now may be different from what worked last year, and it may not work a year from now. Anything to do with Bookfunnel didn't exist a few years ago, for example, and maybe two years from now we'll all be getting books onto devices in a different way, or maybe some other program will come along that serves that same purpose but has some added functionality that will make it the favored method of book delivery. Maybe Amazon will lose the exclusivity requirement to be in

Select (cue me laughing, somehow both hysterically and bitterly at the same time), and we'll have more flexibility with regards to offering free books. Maybe readers will get tired of all these free novellas and we'll have to find something else to give them. We must be flexible and willing to pay attention to current best practices, while still keeping our overall strategy in mind so we can always be employing the most effective tactics that are working *right now*.

In the case of your newsletter (you knew I'd get back to this, right?), your strategy is using reader psychology and purchasing psychology to get people to join your list —and once they're there, to open and click and reply. The myriad ways of accomplishing that goal (the tactics) can change. And, as I said above, they do. All the time.

So let's talk about some strategies and tactics for doing just that, with the understanding that you want to pay special attention to the strategies. You need to be ready to abandon any tactic I might mention, as soon as it stops delivering results for you.

Let's start with the one that will never stop working or being desirable: Organic list-building.

11 - Organic List-Building

SO NOW THAT we understand the crucial difference between strategies and tactics, let's talk about the strategy of organic list-building and empower you to figure out or invent tactics to accomplish that strategy.

This section is very short, because there's not a lot to say about it. You all know what organic list-building is: putting out good books and selling those books to people who will then go on to join your list. The selling part is, of course, way too much to get into here, and the books I recommended earlier will help you with it, but ultimately, you will build the organic part of your list the hard way: one person at a time, on pure merit.

So is it at all possible to give yourself an edge here? Sure! The most important strategy to get people to sign up organically for your list, apart from writing a rip-roaring good book, is *getting visible*. That will never change. Once you have actual readers (which is the very definition of an organic subscriber), your work isn't done.

You have to direct eyeballs to your signup if you want to get anywhere. You need to make sure your readers see that signup link every damn time they turn around.

But how do you do it? That is to say, what *tactics* do you use? Here are a few that work currently:

- Pin it to the top of your Twitter feed (unless you have a new release; during a book launch you want your pinned post to be a link to your new book).
- Put it in your FB header. (Pinned FB posts are actually hidden on mobile so don't do that.)
- Put it in your email signature.
- Calls to action in the back of your books. (If you want your email list to be priority #1— which you almost always do—the mailing list CTA should be the first thing readers see when they finish your book.)
- Facebook group takeovers, blog tours, etc
- Your website (header, footer, sidebar, embedded on the page, or popups. Whatever works).

Now, some of these methods will work better than others, obviously. And some of them will probably always work, while others will fall by the wayside. Maybe Facebook goes belly-up in a year (Lord knows, we'd all get a lot more writing done), who knows? But as long as you understand the strategy—gaining organic visibility with existing readers—you will be able to figure out when certain tactics are no longer working for you, look at that strategy, and devise some new tactics to accomplish the same thing.

All of the preceding items have one thing in common, however: They are all designed to appeal to someone who has heard of you or your books, and comes looking for more—the organic subscribers. That's great and all, but what about the people who haven't heard of you, and don't yet know how awesome you are?

We need to find a way to get them on your list, too, and nothing works so well as a good old-fashioned bribe.

12 - Straight-Up Bribes

NOW, before we discuss the delights and benefits of bribery, I want to take a step back and dig a little deeper into the concept of a loss leader. As I said a couple of chapters ago, having a loss leader is always going to be a winning strategy. But what should you use as a loss leader, and what do you do with it? What should you use to give potential subscribers that free first taste of what you have to offer, literarily speaking, and how do you get them to try it?

What I'm saying is: Let's talk about cookies. (*Finally.*)

Cookies work. I'm not opposed to them; in fact, I believe very strongly that bribing people to join your email list is not only okay but a great way to list-build. However, bribing them with the wrong thing is an absolute disaster—and we see this a lot. I think, again, it comes from the mentality of "throw the widest net you possibly can and get everybody on the list because maybe somebody will buy something someday." That's panic.

That's operating from a place of fear, or a scarcity mindset (if you'll forgive me getting all Tony Robbins on you for a moment). And that gets you the thing I talked about back in Onboarding Basics—a giant list full of people who don't care about you and can't be arsed to open your emails or click your links, all while Mailerlite or whoever is charging you every month for the privilege of having these deadbeats (who probably signed up because they saw something free and thought *why not?*) on your list.

If you want quality subscribers that like the sort of thing you write, and will probably like you, what you need to do is bribe them onto your list with a *good* cookie —something that's aligned well with everything else that you write and aimed squarely at people who buy and read books, particularly your sort of books. And when you get those subscribers, you have to onboard them properly. I recommend that people do what I do; if someone comes to my list through a freebie, the first automation sequence I put them through doesn't offer any more freebies—and it's quite long, with periodic emails stretched over two months. Free-seekers seem to figure out that they're not dealing with someone who's going to give away everything she writes just to keep people on her list, and they tend to show themselves out by the fourth email.

So, if you have to tempt them with a good cookie, the natural question is *What makes a good cookie?* What do you give these new people that will impress them and make them want more? I've included some links that discuss this in the Helpful Links section, but it's worth taking a few minutes to talk about what I've learned over the last few years.

For one thing, if you're giving them something you've written, give them a *complete experience*. I see people offer a free sample or the first ten chapters, or things of that nature, and I think that's a terrible idea. Don't tease. Give them an entire story—a short story, novella, or entire novel—so they know you can not only write an intriguing beginning or sample, but that you can actually wrap up a story in a satisfying fashion. The length of that story is up to you, but I strongly believe it must be complete.

Some people say give subscribers a whole book—and if you have a lot of books, that's a perfectly valid method. If you have a 5-book series, maybe it isn't a huge financial hardship to give away Book 1 to get subscribers, especially if you tend to have good sell-through and you can count on people reading through the rest of the series, or your whole catalog. But there are definite drawbacks to this approach, not least of which is that giving Book 1 to your mailing list does nothing to help sales of Book 1 on the retailers, and if your Book 1 isn't selling on the retailers (particularly on Amazon), its visibility will decline. It's also worth mentioning that this makes your cookie worthless to those organic fans we talked about earlier, the ones who come to you from a back-of-book CTA. They've almost certainly read your Book 1, so why should they sign up for your list?

Some people give Book 2 away to people who sign up from the CTA at the back of Book 1, but I feel that has the same pitfalls as giving away Book 1—with the added issue that if Amazon, which is entirely algorithm-driven, sees that people buy your Book 1 but no one goes on to pick up your Book 2, how visible do you suppose that book is? (Spoiler: not very.) Again, Chris Fox and David Gaughran cover this in the books I recommended in Your Perfect Subscriber.

Some authors have their books enrolled in KDP Select, which means they aren't allowed to make the ebooks available anywhere else, which would preclude them being able to use one of their books as a cookie. On the other hand, there are authors who *could* give their books away, but don't want to give up that income (valid), or don't want to give away an entire book because they don't want to lessen the perceived value of their books (also valid). And some people simply don't have enough books to make this a viable alternative.

Fortunately, there's a much better alternative—at least in my opinion. Bookfunnel did a great series on options for reader magnets; rather than reinvent the wheel there, I'll link to it in the Helpful Links section. But here are some real-life examples I've seen work well:

- A prequel. One author I know has a five-book series available on Amazon, and it's enrolled in KDP Select. His cookie is an exclusive novella that tells the story of how the villain of that series grew up and became the evil bastard we love to hate.
- An epilogue or extended epilogue. This

works especially well in romance, where readers never seem to be able to get enough of that happy ever after, but it really can be done in any genre. Revisit your characters a little (or a long) way in the future and write a few thousand words about what they're up to. Readers who loved those characters will be thrilled to have the opportunity to check in on them.

- A "sideways story." Another author I know uses a short story that takes place alongside the main action of her novel, but is not part of the novel. It's something that happens "offstage," so to speak, between chapters, and the book doesn't suffer for the absence of it. The CTA in the back of the book is "Would you like to hear what happened when X and Y did Z?" and the natural answer, for any reader who enjoyed the book, is *Hell, yes!*

- The first episode of a serial story (if it can stand alone; remember we're aiming for a complete experience here). One of my romance pen names does this, using the first episode of a billionaire serial. That episode, which does stand alone but hopefully leaves everyone wanting more, is not available by itself anywhere other than by joining my mailing list. The complete serial, in one volume, is sold on Amazon and other platforms (and so this first part is not subject to rules about exclusivity).

You can also use an unrelated short story or novella, but if you do, remember that you want to keep it aligned with the other things you write. So if you write Urban Fantasy, don't use a romance novella (duh). But if you write three different kinds of romance—say military, sports, and billionaire—you might be able to use the same cookie across those subgenres.

And best of all? If your cookie is exclusive to your mailing list—if readers can't get it any other way—you will get more signups than if a potential subscriber can get whatever it is somewhere else. I've seen several real-life examples of someone putting a cookie up for sale and watching newsletter signups drop dramatically.

Note: If your cookie would spoil a book, put the offer for that cookie at the *back* of that book. If reading it out of order will be confusing, make sure the offer comes at a point that won't deliver a confusing experience. For example, if one of your cookies is an extended epilogue, you don't want to give that to people who have never heard of you. If it's a sideways story, only offer it in the back of the book during which it took place offscreen. When deciding where and when to offer any specific cookie, ask yourself:

- How does this lead into my catalog?
- Will it entice people to read more?

- Does it make sense out of context, or does it need to come after something else?
- Will people be at risk of reading out of order something that *should* be read in order?

One thing that should factor heavily when you're deciding what cookie to use (or write! Lots of my students end up writing new cookies once they understand what's most effective) is whether it would appeal to readers who have never heard of you, or whether it will only appeal to people who have read some or all of your catalog. If it will appeal to anyone at all, it's an excellent candidate for all kinds of promotions, bundles, and newsletter swaps.

And, lastly, when you're coming up with ideas for cookies, consider things other than books. Fantasy authors might find that giving away maps works well. Thriller author Mark Dawson used to give away a fake intelligence dossier (heavily redacted, of course) on the main character of his flagship series. Or a writer of family sagas might include a genealogical tree.

Basically, no matter what you write, there's probably some sort of non-book bonus that you can think of if you try hard enough—and if you talk to your readers and watch what other authors are doing.

As I mentioned in the Onboarding chapter, some people have a separate cookie for each of their series. This is a great idea, because it gives an entry point for every series, which will naturally result in more signups. You can even create a box set and give away a *collection* of your cookies in hopes that, as people who signed up from one series read through it, they will want to read the other series.

And if you write a new cookie, send that to your existing list, too! They'll love you for it, and be incentivized to stick around because every once in a while they just get a cool freebie from you for no reason at all. Never forget, while you do want to attract new people to your list, your first priority should be treating well the subscribers who are already there. They've stuck with you; reward them whenever you can.

Now let's shift gears and talk about engagement (and re-engagement), so you've got a responsive list to send all these fun surprises to.

13 - Engagement

I CAN'T COUNT the number of complaints I hear—from both incoming students and other author friends—that run along these lines: "I send out an email every time I have a new release, but my open rates just go down and down, and my click rates are even worse. Why are these people on my list if they don't want to buy my books? If they don't want to open the emails, why haven't they unsubscribed?"

There is *so much* wrong with this that I'm going to break it down sentence-by-sentence for you:

I send out an email every time I have a new release, but my open rates just go down and down, and my click rates are even worse.

Okay, so back in the chapter on the sign-up process, I made some snarky remarks about sending newsletters only when you have a new release. If you were wondering what the hell I have against this method, well, I'll tell you.

Sending an email only when you have a new release is, for most people, not an effective strategy at all. I definitely know plenty of people who follow this method, and only a handful have what I would call a successful list—one with subscribers who open and click on their emails regularly.

But as a general rule, if you only send an email when you have a new release, you create for yourself a threefold problem:

First, unless you release very frequently, readers are not hearing from you often enough to keep you at the forefront of their mind. If you release two or three books a year, chances are good you'll have been forgotten by the time you email them again.

Second, you're not emailing often enough to cement your reputation as a good sender. Remember, we spoke briefly about reputation back in The First Date; let me elaborate now.

Your reputation will first be affected by the EMS you choose. Some EMS have quite generous free options; as a result, the sorts of people who do unsavory things with email (and spoil it for the rest of us) or people who are new to their author career (and as a consequence don't have a huge budget for an EMS, and may just not be that good at email) tend to use those services. If your email comes from one of those, it may not be as well-received as an email from one of the other EMS. (I don't necessarily think this is a huge consideration in choosing an EMS, but it's good to be aware of it.) Getting few or no Spam complaints helps reputation, as do good open and click rates, and frequent replies. Basically, as I've been saying, the way subscribers receive and interact with an email from you contributes to your sender reputation.

However, reputation does not last forever. If there's a long window of time between two of your emails, your reputation will decrease, or possible disappear entirely (there's some disagreement about this, among those of us who find that kind of argument exciting). We can't say for certain how long that window is—I've heard people say 30 days, 6 weeks, 2 months, you name it—but we do know it's there. Some folks say it's a hard window and if you go over, you have to start from scratch. Some say it's more like a points system, where you might take a hit in reputation from going over 30 days, but the 4 emails you sent before count, too, so it's only a small ding.

Whatever the interval is or how badly it can damage you, everyone agrees that if you go longer than that, your reputation is harmed in some fashion, and it certainly isn't *improving*. With some subscribers, this isn't a huge deal; if they've been very engaged with you, you've probably become a trusted sender. But if you haven't been getting replies from this person and they haven't whitelisted you, Gmail has nothing other than your (lack of) reputation by which to judge you—and may very well judge you worthy of the Promotions tab.

I'll talk just a bit more about reputation in later chapters, and I've included links to some very good articles in the Helpful Links section. You should definitely check them out.

The third problem with only sending when you have a new release—and perhaps most important of the three, from a fan-building perspective—is that if you choose to do this, your give-to-ask ratio is way out of whack. ("My *what* ratio?" I hear you saying. We'll get to that shortly.) Every time your readers hear from you, you're asking them to do something to benefit you—specifically, to buy your book.

When we get to the whole give-to-ask thing, you'll understand what I mean and why that's bad. For now, suffice it to say that if the only interactions you have with your list are asking them to do something for you, you're going to lose them—and, in my opinion, you deserve to. Mailing only for new releases sounds like a great way to get subscribers but doesn't in fact get you any subscribers that you can leverage effectively when the time *does* come to ask them for something (and it will).

Why are these people on my list if they don't want to buy my books?

This is the big question, isn't it? And there can be a variety of answers.

Maybe you enticed them onto the list with the wrong thing. I see people giving away gift cards and Kindle Fires, and this is a dreadful way to list-build. It won't benefit you in the slightest, because those kinds of things have nothing to do with your books, but lots of people will sign up because people love free stuff. Always make sure your cookies are the sort of thing that will be loved only by people who like your books (or books very much like yours), not by every person who might want an Amazon gift card (by which I mean "every person with an internet connection").

I'd also think about where you got the subscribers. If it was in a big cross-promo or some sort of list-building giveaway—or any situation, really, where they had to exchange their email address to get something free from you—they may very well *not* want to buy your books (yet). They may have joined simply for the free taste and they either haven't gotten around to reading it yet or they weren't interested enough in what they read to continue opening your emails. Fixing (or preventing) this is, as we've discussed, the job of your onboarding sequence. If you're finding that people aren't interacting with emails right after the onboarding—or, worse, emails that are part of your onboarding—you either have a massive deliverability problem or your onboarding isn't doing what it's supposed to.

Sometimes—and oh boy does this one suck—the problem is with the books. If subscribers liked your books when they signed up, but stopped enjoying them, their urge to open your newsletter will wane as well. If you've noticed markedly decreased sales followed by fewer signups and less engagement with current subscribers, you may have a sell-through problem, and that's usually down to something about the books. Figure out where the dropoff is happening and fix the problem. I can't solve that problem here, obviously, but this is the sort of thing that it's great to get someone to help you with—a book doctor or consultant of some kind. Ask fellow authors for recommendations of people who might be able to help you.

(An aside: *Never* take advice from someone who doesn't have a demonstrable track record or great word-of-mouth from authors you know or who are well-respected in the author community—and even then, use your head. If something sounds too good to be true, it probably is. And if someone suggests a solution to an issue you're having, and it makes absolutely no sense, they're probably wrong. Every time in my career that someone has given me really good advice about an issue I was having, it's been like someone turned a light on—"*Of course* that's how to fix it!"—and you should have a similar reaction to any advice you paid for. If you don't, it may not be very good advice.)

If they don't want to open the emails, why haven't they unsubscribed?

That's a fair question. Again, the answer could be one of several things, or even a combination.

They might just not have gotten around to it; I am personally guilty of not unsubscribing until I notice I haven't opened someone's emails in months. And even then it might take me a while to get to it if I'm swamped with other things.

They might be waiting to see if you offer more free

stuff, and not opening because they figure they can deduce from the subject line if you have a freebie for them.

They might actually be opening your emails, but you can't see it. What I mean is, they might be reading email in such a way that the open doesn't register with your EMS. Some people read in Microsoft Outlook's preview pane, for example, which does not register as an open. Many people turn off images to conserve data if they read on their phones, and some email providers—Gmail, for example—disable images by default in many emails, particularly ones it determines are marketing-related. EMS like MailChimp use an invisible image to tell them if someone has opened an email. If the image doesn't load, you don't know that the subscriber opened your email. You can get around this by making them click— clicks always register—but some people refuse to click on links in emails, and there's very little you can do about that. When the time comes to re-engage people who aren't opening and/or clicking (more on that in a moment), you'll have to use some special techniques for folks like that.

The second thing to consider is that they might very much like to open your emails, but that they simply aren't seeing them. Delivery is a real problem, and only becoming more difficult. So let's take a few minutes to talk about deliverability—or lack thereof.

14 - Deliverability

DELIVERABILITY—DEFINED here as the likelihood that your emails will be delivered to the inboxes of subscribers, rather than flagged as Spam or Promotions— is inextricably linked to engagement. Basically, you need to keep people engaged if you want them to continue to see your emails, but you need them to see your emails if you want to keep them engaged. It's a real chicken-or-egg situation, and no one wants their livelihood dependent on a causality dilemma, so you want to start engaging them right from the start, as we talked about before, and you want to make sure that they understand they need to be proactive about looking for your emails. (You see why I bang on so endlessly about whitelisting?) One thing I find effective is to post on Facebook and Twitter when I've sent out a newsletter, so that subscribers who see the post might go look for theirs. It's not foolproof (because visibility on social media is universally pretty rubbish), but every open helps.

Deliverability is going down for lots of people; if you're seeing this, you are not alone.

When you send, Gmail (or Hotmail, or whomever) decides what to do with your email. Mostly, it seems they decide that the one thing they should definitely not do is show it to the person who asked for it. There are a few reasons.

For one thing, email providers are getting tougher in the way that they evaluate emails. Things that would have passed a Spam filter no problem a year ago will send up red flags now, and prevent you from reaching inboxes. I'm talking here about things like lots of links in the email, too many—or any!—images, too many exclamation points, certain words or types of links, etc. I've included some links in the Helpful Links section that will help you to avoid Spam filters. But this is something that changes over time, and you'll need to keep yourself educated about what sorts of things may trigger a red flag. It's worth making a note to yourself to Google a couple of times a year and see if something you've been doing for a while might now be negatively affecting your deliverability.

Additionally, actions you take can also affect your deliverability. As we've discussed, getting people to whitelist you will affect it positively. Sending boring, too-frequent, or inappropriate newsletters will lead to decreased engagement, which leads to deliverability issues. Do not send boring emails, ever. Even one really bad email can cause a huge dip in opens the next time you send.

And, finally, readers just have newsletter fatigue. This, again, leads to non-opens, which leads to poor deliverability. The solution to this is to have a newsletter that is so uniquely you that it will without question be something your readers look forward to—because they like you, remember? Be yourself, and they will like your newsletter as well.

So, assuming you're writing decent emails and not doing spammy things, how do you convince Gmail or whomever that they should be delivering your emails instead of routing them to the circular file? You do this by making damn sure that those people who *do* see your emails interact with them in the ways we've talked about, thereby raising your reputation and increasing the likelihood that further emails from you will not be judged as harshly. In a perfect world, after a period of time where you've proved yourself to be a wonderful sender with lots of engagement, you would somehow become safe, or see no declines. This is not that world.

The sad truth is, you will absolutely see a decline in open rates over the lifetime of your list. Always. No matter how good your emails are, no matter how carefully cultivated your list, open rates will decline, because the deck is stacked against you. And then every email that doesn't get opened only confirms the email providers' bad opinion of you, which leads to more of your emails not reaching their destination, and now we're back to a chicken-and-egg thing.

You will fight for deliverability throughout the entire

life of your newsletter, and I imagine it's only going to get more difficult as time goes on. You'll want to stay on top of this topic, for sure, and be ready to pivot when things change.

So, knowing all this—and feeling hopeless now that I've been such a Debbie Downer—how do we increase deliverability when we see that ours is declining?

Before we talk about the answer, let's talk about what's *not* the answer: getting more subscribers.

Don't misunderstand me; you want to be getting new subscribers steadily, from whatever sources you've determined work well for you. I'm not saying abandon list-building or anything crazy like that. But *new* subscribers aren't going to do much for your deliverability; you have no history with them, and no reputation related to communication between the two of you. In fact, when you look at it that way, new subscribers are, in the short-term, more likely to give you a slight decrease in visibility. They are not the answer to this particular problem.

So how *do* you increase deliverability?

The first step is to start absolutely *nailing* this whole newsletter thing. This means building relationships and delivering value. We'll hit those in the next two chapters.

The second step is to be constantly re-engaging the list you already have, which is the chapter after that.

And finally, once you've done your best to get people's attention and given them great reasons to stick around and keep opening, you're going to use the information in the last chapter to toss all the dead weight overboard.

We're in the home stretch now.

15 - Building Relationships

SO THE FIRST order of business is building genuine, two-way relationships with your subscribers, which is neither as scary nor as difficult as it seems. This is where you start differentiating your list from everyone else's and getting your subscribers to stick to you like glue.

Now that we've got a handle on deliverability (I will never call that particular problem *solved*, but "got a handle on it" seems okay), we can think about the purpose of your emails. As I think I've made clear, selling books is a secondary purpose, but primarily you are building that list of superfans that I keep waxing rhapsodic about. To do that—to truly cement those readers to you and turn them into the kind of fans who go out and evangelize about you—you need to take it to the next level. And that starts with building actual relationships with your subscribers.

This chapter is another long one, because this is a real sticking point for many people. Of all the things I teach in Mailing List Expert, I think this is the point on which I get the most pushback from students. For many people, this step seems like the hardest of all; fortunately, it's not. It's actually quite easy once you understand two things: *why* you're doing it, and *how* to do it.

The *why* is simple; as I've said before (and will say again, probably so much that you'll have nightmares about it), you are creating a fanbase. Selling books is a happy side effect of that, but creating that fanbase *must* be your primary objective—because one will lead to the other, but only in one direction. I'm putting this next thing in its own paragraph, because it's the bedrock of my entire philosophy, which by this point I dearly hope you've bought into:

Not everyone who buys one of your books will become a lifelong fan, but *your lifelong fans will buy all of your books.*

Do you see how powerful that is? I can't stress it enough. Don't direct your newsletter's focus solely (or even mainly) on selling whatever book you happen to be flogging today; build superfans and they will buy the book you have out today, and the one you have in two months, and all the ones after that—without you having to *sellsellsell* to a group of folks who might shrug and decide they're just not that into you.

Trying to get a group of mildly interested people to buy your new release is no way to sell books, and it's *not* what your mailing list should be about. Your mailing list is a two-way street, and the only way you're going to get traffic going both ways on that street is to get your subscribers to have conversations with you. You do this by building relationships. (Man, I am really sorry that I'm using the phrase "building relationships" so much. You'd think it was crucial or something!)

And in the long run, you will be saving yourself a ton of effort, because an engaged list of lifelong, rabid fans will respond to your release notices *en masse*, and that's a hell of a lot easier—and more fun—than having to go out and find readers with every new book, hoping to get it to sell well. Instead of replicating all that work with every release, put your effort into turning the readers who find you casually into superfans who wait impatiently for your new release email, and let them make you a bestseller purely because they love you.

As for the *how*, the best way—I would argue the only way—to build those relationships is to get to know your subscribers and let them get to know you. Let's tackle the simplest one first.

Getting to Know Your Subscribers

Getting to know your subscribers is a complete no-brainer once you think about it. You do it by asking good questions that effectively solicit replies, and answering the emails you receive as a result. So simple, so easy, so powerful. (And so time-consuming, but we'll address that later—or, as I like to say, "That's a problem for future Tammi." She *hates* me.)

What qualifies as a "good question"? What sort of question effectively solicits replies? This is, to some degree, one of those "it depends" things. The answers may vary depending on your genre, subgenre, subscribers, list-building techniques, onboarding ... there are so many variables.

My advice is to split-test (how surprising). Send two versions of the same question, each to half the list, and see which gets the most responses. Use that information to formulate two questions you can split-test in your next campaign. If you continue on in this vein (and track the answers, so you're actually evaluating the data instead of going by what you kind of remember from three campaigns ago), you'll eventually have a keen understanding of what sorts of things get your subscribers talking to you (and if you also have a Facebook or other reader group, they'll start talking to *each other*, which is also very powerful).

So, to some degree, you're going to have to figure out for yourself what makes a good question. But I can give you some general guidelines.

Good questions:

- **are actually questions.** I know that seems ridiculously basic, but "Don't you think friends-to-lovers is the best romance trope?" is a statement disguised as a question. Don't do that. "What's your favorite romance trope?" is going to start a much better dialogue.
- **are open-ended.** "Who is the most

handsome actor working right now?" will get more (and better) responses than "Ryan Gosling or Ryan Reynolds?"

- **don't have a "right" answer.** "What superhero movie do you love most?" works better than "What was the first movie in the new Marvel Cinematic Universe?"

- **are free of bias.** "Are you tired of all the terrible books in the Kindle Store?" presupposes that there are in fact a lot of terrible books in the Kindle Store. "Are you able to find books you enjoy when shopping the Kindle Store?" will certainly reveal to you the people who think the store is full of terrible books, but it also leaves the question open to those who don't think that.

- **are positive in tone.** One other problem with the question above is that it's inherently negative. Even were it not biased, it just makes me crabby to read it. All those terrible books, after all. So phrase your questions in a way that invites positivity: "What was the best book you read last year?" as opposed to "What book do you absolutely hate?"

- **encourage longer and more specific answers.** "What's your favorite reality TV show?" is fine, but "What's your favorite reality TV show, and why?" is better. (And "What's your favorite reality TV show, and what do you love about it?" is better yet, because it combines this rule with the preceding positivity rule.)

- **are relevant to what you write about.** "When you were a child, what did you want to be when you grew up?" is a great question for the mailing list of a non-fiction author who talks about goals or fulfillment; not so much for someone who writes Motorcycle Club romance. Meanwhile, the MC romance folks will have enthusiastic answers to "Who's your favorite characters in Sons of Anarchy?" (spoiler: the answer will *always* be "Jax." You're welcome), while some if not all of the non-fiction audience will have no idea what you're even talking about.

- **address topics that people can get excited about.** "What's your favorite soda?" is, in my opinion, a pretty boring question. I mean, I even *have* a favorite soda, but I can't imagine getting passionate about it. But ask me who's the best Golden Girl, and you'll get a four-page, point-by-point dissertation. (It's Dorothy, go ahead and fight me.)

There are a lot of other things that would define a "good question," but that list is a pretty good place to start. I've included a few great resources in the Helpful

Links section—sites that list great getting-to-know-you questions—but you can also just Google something like "conversation starters" or "good questions to ask" and find hundreds of sites you can use to spark ideas. And, as always, your own list is going to guide you in what works and what doesn't. Track everything—open rates, click rates, response rates, unsubscribes—and use that data to determine what turns your readers off and what keeps them coming back for more.

As I've said a bunch of times, when people open and click your emails, this signals to their email provider that they are interested in the content, which does wonders for your reputation as a sender. But your reputation will improve even more if people *reply* to your emails— because when they do, they are *having a conversation* with you, and there's nothing email providers like more than conversations. Replies tell the email provider that this is a wanted email, that you are a trusted sender, that you are someone the receiver wants to hear from and communicate with.

Getting replies to your campaigns is one of the best techniques there is for staying out of the Spam folder or Promotions tab. Believe it, internalize it, use it mercilessly. Hone your questions to razor sharpness, polish them like diamonds, and send them out there into the world to tempt readers like the devil tempted Eve (though with considerably less catastrophic results, one hopes).

So by asking a good question that elicited a reply, you've:

- softened up the person you're talking to
- established a connection with them
- asked them to tell you something about themselves, and
- as a side benefit, increased your reputation with their email provider.

Not a bad return on the time investment necessary to think of a compelling question.

Now, I'm sure some of you are asking, "Does this mean I have to reply to all those emails?" It depends, but my general answer is *yes*, in many cases you will have to—or want to!—reply to those emails. I know we're all pressed for time, so that can seem daunting, but I meant it when I said this is a two-way street.

The good news is, when you're just starting out, not many people will answer. I'm sure you can find time to answer a handful of emails, and if you're only emailing once a month, you can probably even answer a few hundred replies to each newsletter. When you're at the point where every email gets so many replies you literally can't keep up, that's a quality problem to have; you've got a crazy engaged list and can almost certainly afford to hire someone to handle them for you. Barring that, you can streamline replying if you just reuse the same answers where possible.

Let me give you an example of what I mean. In a recent campaign, I asked my subscribers who their favorite superhero was. Lots of folks replied (far more than I expected, which was wonderful). I manage my pen name's email in Gmail, so I'm able to use Gmail's canned responses feature. I set up canned responses as I got replies, and thereafter if someone gave me an answer I'd already seen, I just plopped the same text into my reply. For example, everyone who chose Thor (and that was seriously 80% of them) got a reply that said "You won't be surprised to hear that he took an early and decisive lead." Typing that, or some variation of it, to the several hundred people who gave me that answer, would have been a waste of time—and, frankly, tedious. With the canned response, it took only a few seconds per email, and everyone felt they got a genuine response. And honestly? They *did* get a genuine response. I read every email and sent them a reply that was what I would have written anyway, without having to take the time to compose that same reply over and over again. (I did have to write a unique reply for the woman who chose He-Man—she was a singular event—but our conversation about how she was the only one to make that choice was funny, and you can bet your ass that she'll be buying my superhero romance.)

The same principle applies even if you're not using Gmail; just use typing shortcuts or a document file that you can use for cut-and-paste answers. However you do it, the ultimate return on that time investment is so high that it's well worth it.

The beauty of this approach—asking open-ended, positive, relevant, interesting questions that engage readers and encourage dialogue—is that when subscribers reply (and they will), a couple of cool things happen to the relationship between you.

First, that subscriber is no longer some faceless entity passively receiving your emails. They've replied to you. Their name is there in your inbox. Their answer to your question tells you something about them. And just the fact that they took the time to answer at all means that they like you, or that you asked a good question, or both. This is exactly what you're trying to build, one subscriber at a time.

Second, when you reply to them, they learn a little about you; this makes them more disposed to pick up your next book, more likely to recommend you to a friend. You've come to know them a bit, but they've also come to know you, and that personal connection is the difference between a casual reader and a ride-or-die fan.

This is what I mean when I say email is a two-way street. This isn't about sending information to your list. This is about dialogue, and getting to know one another. And yes, that means your subscribers need to know you, too.

Being Authentic

Let me stress: as I've said a couple of times, this does *not* mean you have to reveal anything about yourself that makes you uncomfortable. Subscribers, like everyone else in your life, will know precisely what you allow them to know. Your spouse, if you have one, probably knows a great deal about you; your coworkers at your day job, maybe (hopefully!) not so much. Your Facebook "friends" that you haven't actually seen since high school? Very little. (Well, they know about your misspent youth, but probably not so much about the real you *now*.)

So please don't think I'm saying you have to tell your subscribers your hopes and dreams, your darkest secrets, or anything about your family. You get to decide which things are for public consumption and which are not.

Some of my students just don't care about privacy; they send baby pictures, reveal their personal struggles, talk about sex—all manner of things that you might consider too private. There's nothing wrong with that. That's who they are, that's probably reflected in their books, and it's perfectly appropriate for their particular mailing list.

But if you're a more reticent type, there are lots of things you can tell your subscribers that give them a glimpse of you without violating whatever boundaries you set.

You do need to be genuine. I say "Be your authentic self" so frequently in MLE that my students have probably all developed a nervous tic about it. Hell, I've used it quite a few times right here in this book. Maybe I'll try to cut back.

But being yourself does not mean that you have to tell people sacred things. You are, one hopes, a well-rounded human being, with many and varied interests and habits, and any one of your many interesting facets is fodder for newsletter chatter.

What kind of movies do you like? What's the most

recent movie you saw, and what did you think of it? What's your favorite movie? What movie didn't live up to your expectations? What movie are you looking forward to?

What books did you love as a child? What books made you want to be a writer? What's the best book you've ever read (yes, go out on a limb and pick *one*—it's a good exercise anyway)? What book are you reading right now?

What's your favorite food? What's one food you like that no one else seems to? What's one food everyone is gaga over that you wouldn't put in your mouth for a million dollars? What food are you great at cooking at home? What food can't you cook no matter how many times you've tried?

What TV shows did you love growing up? Did any of them inform your writing even though they were in a different medium? What are you watching these days that you're willing to admit to? Which ones are a guilty pleasure? Which show do you think was canceled too soon, and which show do you think dragged on way too long?

What do you *really* think about social media? If you love it, why, and what do you say to people who think it's stupid? If you hate it, are you there anyway, and why? Which platforms do you like? Which do you hate?

(Confession: it was incredibly hard for me not to answer every one of the above questions in parentheses. You're welcome.)

I'll stop there rather than belabor the point, which is:

there are plenty of things that are appropriate for social interaction without giving out your SSN and mother's maiden name. And depending on genre, you might have a wealth of topics that are unique to your subscribers. Romance writers can ask which Chris is the hottest—Pine, Pratt, Evans, or Hemsworth? (It's Hemsworth.) Science fiction writers can share recent articles on the topic of time travel or gene manipulation or space exploration, depending on which sub-genre of SF they write. Writers of historical fiction can share interesting things they discover during their research. Urban fantasy writers can opine about how much relationship stuff and/or sexytimes makes a book Paranormal Romance rather than UF. And so on.

In short (which clearly I'm not good at), there are folks who let it all hang out, and folks who would prefer to keep walls (and maybe a moat) around some things. No matter which one you are, there are many things that you can share, ask, or hold forth about that will respect whatever boundaries you've set around your personal life, no matter how strict or forgiving those boundaries are. You can reveal things to your readers that will get them to identify with you, without feeling like you've violated yourself.

Just be yourself. (See, I didn't say "be your authentic self"—except I just did. Damn it!)

Oh, and one more thing: You can't use these techniques disingenuously, because it will backfire on you. Most readers can tell a phony from a mile away, and I know very few authors who can carry off a persona that's wildly different from their actual self, at least not for long. But if you use these best practices (in a genuine way), you will build that list of superfans I keep banging on about.

Because remember: we are building superfans, not casual readers. The superfans will help you reach the casual readers, if you amass enough of them and treat them well. And you will, because as we move into the next chapter we're going to address one of the most difficult parts of this whole newsletter game: delivering value in each and every email you send.

16 - Delivering Value

OKAY, deliver value. Sounds great, right. But *how* do you deliver value?

Delivering value can mean a number of things—sharing articles or videos that fans will enjoy, sneak peeks at your work in progress, cover reveals, pictures of your cat (yes, everyone loves this, and no, I can't explain it), book recommendations … the list goes on and on, and encompasses just about everything you can do with a newsletter.

There's something missing from that list, though, isn't there? There's nothing there about getting them to buy your books.

You're right; there isn't.

Because you need to stop thinking about yourself.

I'll give you a second to take that in—because chances are good that most people who talk to you about how to run your email list talk to you about how to convert to sales, how to get people to do what you tell them to do and click on what you want them to click on. Most people talk to you about your email list as though your email list is expected to perform for you.

If you want to have a crazy-successful mailing list, you need to turn that completely on its head.

This isn't about you.

I know that's tough to get your head around. *Of course* this is about you. If you don't sell books, you don't make a living. But as I said way back at the beginning of this book (and something like five hundred times since), your list is not for selling books. Your list is for selling yourself. Your list is for building superfans—and superfans, by definition, will buy your books.

You do not build superfans by expecting your list to say "how high?" every time you say "jump." Instead, give them something to jump for. And you need to give it to them much more often than you ask for something in return. I call this the *give-to-ask ratio*.

The Give-to-Ask Ratio

Let's start with definitions. A *give* is something of value that you give (duh) to your subscribers, free and clear—a short story you wrote, a link to a free or sale-priced book they might like, a picture of Jason Momoa, whatever. An *ask* is, to the surprise of absolutely no one, a request for your subscribers to do something for you—buy your book, vote in a poll, leave a review, etc.

You need to keep the give-to-ask ratio at the forefront of your mind when you're planning and composing campaigns—and, for that matter, your autoresponders, though I would say that any ask in an autoresponder should be a *very* soft ask (no hard sells, nothing labor-intensive). You'll find a ratio that's comfortable for you, but keep in mind that it should *heavily* favor the subscriber rather than you. You are competing with countless other authors, all vying for subscriber attention; make sure that your list is the one they wouldn't dream of unsubscribing from.

The give-to-ask ratio doesn't have to be a specific formula, like "For every ask you must first have three gives." You *can* have a formula if you like, if that helps you to police yourself and make sure you're keeping an eye on it. But if you're the sort who can just kind of feel that you've been good about not asking for things for a while and now would be a fine time to do so, go right ahead and keep it informal. Whatever works for you.

One thing that will help a lot with that give-to-ask ratio is keeping your release emails completely separate from your regular newsletter. For example, my newsletter goes out with an attractive header, a give or two, and unobtrusive, in-line sales links if I mention one of my books, but there's no overt direction to go buy something. We're just talking, my subscribers and me, and I'm not going to ruin our nice conversation with a bunch of slick sales talk. But when I have a new book, readers get an email from me that doesn't look like my newsletter; it's stripped-down, no header, few or no pictures, just a short and sweet "The new book's out, here's a link, go get it."

So if you email every other Friday, or on the 15th of

every month, or whatever your schedule is, do that as promised. Then, on release day—whether that's every month or every three months, or whatever—send them the release email. This email doesn't count as your once-a-month (or however often) newsletter, because (she said for the millionth time) the purpose of your newsletter isn't to sell books. Selling is different than talking to your people, and if you can divorce those two things, you will be solid.

I do it this way for a couple of reasons. One, I want my newsletter to feel a little like getting an email from a friend. Now obviously my subscribers and I aren't friends in any traditional sense, but I want them to get something akin to the warm fuzzies when they see my name in their inbox. Keeping sales emails to a completely different format and not replacing the regular newsletter with a sales email lets the reader know that I like them quite apart from trying to sell them books.

And, it's worth pointing out, those stripped-down release emails are less likely to trigger Spam flags, so the open rates on my release emails tend to be 10-12% higher than any individual newsletter open rate. That's a win right there.

This will usually keep your give-to-ask ratio well in hand, because almost no one I know is publishing books so fast that they would send more release emails than newsletters. So the pattern will automatically set you up for more give interactions than ask ones. People worry a lot about not having enough to talk about between books, but I promise, you have plenty to talk about. Just the lists of question in the last chapter will keep you busy for ages, and if you Google "conversation starters" like I recommended, you could probably write a weekly email even if you only release once a year and never make your subscribers feel like you were wasting their time. And that, of course, is the one thing we must never, ever do. Respect your subscribers' time and treat them well; it will build goodwill, and then those subscribers are there for you when you need them.

Treating Your Subscribers Well

So, how do you do that—treat your subscribers well? What can you do to make your newsletter something readers don't just welcome, but look for and are excited about? Aside from keeping your give-to-ask ratio in mind, there are some other principles that will help you make your newsletter a great experience that keeps them coming back for more.

- *Ask yourself, before each email you send, "What's in this for my subscriber?"* If there's nothing exciting, interesting, or notable about the email you're about to send, don't send it! Respect your subscribers' time by making sure they're always glad they opened your newsletter, because there was something in it for them. That's the one thing no email can be without.
- *Make your subscribers feel special.* They're

your fans, which makes them part of a community of people who love your work. Even if that's a community of ten, so what? Always treat your list the same—as though you're honored that they chose to spend time with your newsletter—no matter what size it is. (And remember, your subscriber avatars come in handy here.)

- *Make it so good they recommend it to their friends.* New books, deals, book recommendations, funny memes, cool research, travel diaries, pet pictures … always and forever with the pet pictures. If you're constantly delivering laughs or feels or great recommendations or whatever it is that your subscribers love, they're going to tell their friends "You've got to sign up for this; it's awesome."

- *Only send them relevant emails.* As I mentioned in The Sign-Up Process, this is a great time to start tagging or segmenting people. Higher-end EMS like Drip and ActiveCampaign and ConvertKit will allow you to set tags that will be applied when a subscriber takes a certain action, and that allow you to sort out groups of people to target with specific emails. Other EMS have similar, if slightly less robust, options like segments and groups.

Let me take a break from the list for a second, and give you an example of a good thing to select for: In the last email of my romance pen name's onboarding sequence, I list the major ebookstores (Amazon, iBooks, Kobo, B&N, and Google Play, at the time of this writing) and ask subscribers to click whichever platform they prefer to shop on; there's also a "No Preference" option. In this way, I can be sure not to send Kobo readers emails about books that might only be available on Amazon or iBooks.

You can also sort of jerry-rig this stuff with the less expensive options, but you have to consider the balance between spending your time on something or spending your money. As with so many things in indie publishing, when you're starting out, you probably have more time than money, and it makes sense to bootstrap what you can and DIY as much as possible. But as money becomes more plentiful, the value of your time will increase, and there usually comes a point where paying for convenience or assistance is worth it. You'll know when that time comes.

Okay, back to ways to treat your subscribers well:

- *Don't be spammy.* This should go without saying, but I'll say it anyway. Don't be one of those people who does so many newsletter swaps you're sending an email to your list every day. Don't recommend books you haven't read (or otherwise know to be good, like ones from a favorite author that you know never disappoints). Don't resend an unopened email more than once. Don't email the non-openers asking why they don't like you anymore. Remember what you told people they were signing up for, and only give them that. That's all you have permission for, really.

- *Solicit replies in every email.* Building a two-way relationship with subscribers makes you feel like a real person to them, someone they know, and they're more likely to continue opening your emails and deepening that connection.

- *Give readers what they want.* How do you know what they want? You ask them. Ask them either/or questions, poll them, make suggestions and tell them to reply and let you know what they think. They will absolutely weigh in on the things that matter to them.

And, of course, as a bonus (everyone knows what's coming, but I'll say it anyway): When you do those things and people respond by opening, clicking, replying, you improve your reputation.

Also, keep in mind that anything you send that's relevant to you and your work—especially cover reveals, sneak peeks, excerpts, and the like—is a powerful form of *selling without selling*. Hyping up your work by letting subscribers in on the creative process, in large or small ways, gets them excited for the release day, and means they're looking for that email that says "The book is finally here!" Ultimately, good marketing is about putting a product or service in front of the people most likely to want it. This is exactly what you're doing with your newsletter.

And for the people who *don't* seem to be excited about the new book, or your newsletter, or even you? The ones who don't open, click, or reply? First, you try to bring them back into the fold (re-engagement); if that doesn't work, you dump them (purge the dead weight) without remorse.

Let's start with re-engagement.

17 - Re-engagement

RE-ENGAGEMENT IS the process of identifying the people who aren't interacting with your emails and targeting them with specific campaigns designed to get them opening, clicking, and replying again. In my opinion, all engagement is really about *re*-engagement, because the people who are opening and clicking and replying aren't the ones who need to be engaged; they're not the problem. The people who have whitelisted you are *really* not the problem. The problem is the people who are simply not opening your emails. You've got them; we all do, and that's just the way of things. The key is to try to weed those people out whenever possible, so they're not hanging around like so much dead weight, screwing up your open rates and causing the people who *do* want your emails not to see them.

But first we want to make sure that either they really don't want to hear from us or, for whatever reason, they aren't seeing our emails and we can't overcome it. Sometimes you won't be able to tell which, because they look the same: someone is sent your re-engagement campaign and never opens. But in the end it doesn't really matter which camp they fall into; if you can't get them to open an email, out they go. The interval is up to you, of course, but I try to re-engage and purge twice a year.

So how *do* we get them to open emails, when by definition they haven't been for a while now? By taking what we know about how to craft killer emails and turning it up to eleven. (Oh, man, I really hope I'm not the only one who gets that reference.)

What?

I hear you. You're already doing your best, writing emails that would make angels weep (if angels cared about emails, which they don't), delivering value in every paragraph, every sentence, every semicolon; and here I come to tell you to work *harder*.

Yeah. I'm like that. But take heart; it's not hopeless, and I'm not actually telling you to work harder. I'm telling you to work *differently*. There are specific methods to re-engage people who have fallen by the wayside, and they're actually not the same ones that you use to keep month-to-month engagement with the section of your list that's responsive.

The first—and probably most important—part of your re-engagement campaign is writing absolutely irresistible subject lines.

Now, obviously you should have been writing great subject lines all along; I've chosen to put it in this chapter because even though they're important to every email (and you should be making them as good as you can, every time), the engaged portion of your list, as I mentioned above, is not causing you trouble. They'll forgive you if your subject line isn't honed to diamond-like brilliance. But here, among people who seem not to care about you, you really need your subject lines to shine.

Remember, you're dealing with *non-openers*, so you absolutely cannot rely on the content of the newsletter to do the work of re-engaging. You have to grab them with the subject line—to the point where, even though they have been ignoring your emails for a while, they simply have to open this one.

In the Helpful Links section, I've linked to some really excellent articles on how to create great subject lines, but let's also talk about it a bit here. Subject lines are at once one of the easiest things to do and one of the hardest. Easy, because you know how to entertain people and get their attention; you're a writer, for crying out loud. But hard, because subject lines can be tricky, and the advice you get about them is pretty much always contradictory. They need to be descriptive, but not too long, especially now that everyone is reading on their phones and only sees a little bit of the subject line. They need to be straightforward, so people know what they're getting, but also intriguing, so they want to open. If they're time-sensitive, you want to say so, but you don't want to sound like that store that's had a "Going out of business sale" for the last 3 years. Being funny helps a lot, but you can't be too weird or it'll put people off.

No problem, right?

But some best practices are universal. Make your subject lines relevant to the content inside. Make them catchy. Give people a reason to open—a benefit or surprise or mystery. Ask a question. If you can get a very short quote from a testimonial, those work great.

Interestingly, numbers seem to increase open rates. "The 10 best books I read last year," for example, or "5 authors that are automatic release-day buys for me."

Giving someone a command rather than just declaring information works well; "Get my new release today!" as opposed to "My new book is here!"

Seasonal things are always a hit. If you're a romance writer who doesn't send a special email around Valentine's Day, or a horror writer who's not taking full advantage of Halloween, then you are really asleep at the switch and need to up your game.

Puns! People freaking *love* puns, and just wordplay in general. So if you can be clever—or so cringe-worthy that it circles back around to being clever again—go for it.

And one weird thing (ha! See what I did there?) that works like gangbusters is emojis—particularly the poop emoji. Yes, it's true; in terms of increasing open rates, the poop emoji outperforms all other emojis by a notable margin. (There's a link to an article about this in the Helpful Links section.)

The poop emoji is probably not appropriate for what

you're writing (but if it is, whatever, you do you), but other emojis also increase open rates. If you can relate them to the subject of the email, or just to your genre, tone, or theme in general, subscribers are quite responsive to that as well—hearts for romance authors, for example, or a robot for science fiction.

You definitely want to be aware of what words will get you flagged as Spam (both in the subject line and in the email itself, actually); we talked about this in the chapter on Deliverability. But you also have to understand that you are in fact selling books, and you are in fact sometimes giving something away, and if you have to say that in plain language then that's just how it is. Fortunately, since you've been working so hard to build a great reputation and encourage whitelisting, and all that good stuff we've been talking about, your deliverability can take the small hit that comes with using the words "gift card" or "free" or whatever.

And you want to split-test *everything*. You can test some really general things, like whether your subscribers are more likely to open if the subject line references a popular movie, or if books get a better response instead. But you can also get really granular with this, and split-test subject lines that differ in some very small way; for example, "You have to read this book!" vs "You have to buy this book!" (The first one's going to work better. There, I saved you a split-test.)

When you begin your re-engagement campaign, though, all of that flies out the window. There's really only one rule at the start of re-engagement: The subject line needs to make it clear that there is something *really good* inside, and that it's not going to cost them a cent. It's that simple. Make them absolutely *have* to open, and give them a really great freebie that no sane person could resist clicking on.

If they click, great. They move on to the next part of the sequence, and—this is the important part—no more freebies for them. The next email can offer an inexpensive book, even 99 cents if you've got one to offer or know of one you can recommend, but you aren't going to send any more freebies to this campaign. The freebie was solely to get their attention; now that you have it, you're going to determine if this is the sort of person who ever clicks on something that might cost them money. If they don't click on your next few emails, don't open them, or didn't even open the first one, they're deadbeats and they have to go. We'll talk about how to get rid of them, but first I need to address a special kind of non-opener that you need to treat better than these deadbeats— because in this case, *you* were the deadbeat.

Special Case: When You're the Reason They're Not Engaged

Sure, sometimes people aren't opening your emails because they're not engaged or they're busy or they're free-seekers or … you know, a million reasons. But sometimes subscribers are unresponsive because *you* weren't handling them right. Maybe you only email when you have a new release, and you only release one book a year. Or maybe you got caught up in newsletter swapping and alienated subscribers by sending emails too frequently. There are a few different ways you can turn off your list—and they will get you a lot of unsubscribes, but some people will stay on the list, hoping that it might be good again.

If you have existing lists like this—ones that are fallow or that you haven't been treating right—you re-engage them like any other non-opener (with a crazy good email they can't resist opening). But once they've opened that first re-engagement email, you want to shift them into a short little sequence (similar to your onboarding sequence) where you re-orient them to you, your books, and your newsletter; and where you make it clear that this newsletter is about to become *awesome*, so they should give you another chance.

If you're making changes to the frequency of your newsletter, this is a great time to tell them that. If you have something to apologize for, just do it. You'll win some people back by saying "I didn't know how to do this newsletter thing right so I was doing XYZ, and that's not any fun for you," and the people you can't win back weren't going to love you again anyway. Treat it like any other relationship you screwed up: say you're sorry, try to fix it, and then move on if you have to, wiser and determined never to make that mistake again.

Just bring them back into the fold with two or three

emails to give them an idea of what they can expect from you *now*, and dump them back into your regular list.

And then any who weren't responsive from this group or the other group(s) is going over the side like so much ballast. It's time to purge the dead weight, folks.

18 - Purging Dead Weight

THIS IS GOING to be pretty short and straightforward, because this topic is exceedingly simple. As we discussed a few chapters ago, people who don't open or interact with your emails hurt your overall deliverability, to the point where even people who do interact with your emails will start to see fewer of them. Weed them out ruthlessly—you *must* be ruthless here, because you are protecting your relationship with the subscribers who *do* want to hear from you.

Weed them out? But how? How do you know which subscribers to keep and which to get rid of? It's actually not that hard; you find anyone who hasn't opened a certain number of your recent emails (a number you've determined) or who hasn't clicked on anything in a certain number of emails (again determined by you), and you get ready to give them the boot.

All of the mailing list services will let you query your database of subscribers to see who has interacted with your emails in whatever way. (The method is different for every service; consult the Help section or Customer Service if you can't figure out how to do this.) You can ask who didn't open the last email, or the last 5 emails, or several specific emails. You can ask who has clicked on anything in a certain email or emails, or who has clicked on a specific link or links. Basically, you can isolate anyone who isn't doing what you want your subscribers to do.

Once you've identified them, what do you do with them? This part is about as simple as it gets. You give them a chance to stay, and then you boot them, without remorse.

What this means is you'll send what we can call a "Do you want to stay?" email (only one; any more than that is too much effort for very little reward). A "Do you want to stay?" email needs to say a few things:

- you've noticed (or your mailing list service has told you, or however you want to phrase it) that the subscriber hasn't been opening your emails
- you don't want to send emails to people who aren't interested
- you will unsubscribe them unless they click on a link (which you can set up just to go to a dummy page on your site that says "Your click has been recorded" or something) or send you a reply

Anyone who clicks *will* register as an open; all the services are smart enough to figure out that someone who clicks obviously opened the email, even if they didn't register the open for any of the reasons we've discussed previously. You should then tag those people—as well as anyone who replies to you—so you know going forward that your service reports their activity inaccurately, and you don't have to bother sending them future "Do you want to stay?" emails. The number of people in that situation will be quite small, and asking them constantly if they're still there is annoying. That way lies madness.

Subscribers who don't interact with your "Do you want to stay?" email get unsubscribed after whatever period of time you set out in the email. No exceptions and no regrets. You need subscribers who want to be on your list, and who show it by opening, clicking, and replying. You do not need to pay your mailing list service for dead weight that isn't interested in you.

This can sometimes mean culling a large number of people, particularly if you don't do it regularly. Suck it up, cupcake, and do it anyway. (And then come sit by us oldsters and talk about the great GDPR debacle of 2018; it'll make your wound look like a paper cut.) Whatever sales you lose from removing the few people who *might* have come around and begun opening your emails again is more than offset by the net gain in open and click rates, and the subsequent positive effects on your reputation as a sender. Just tell yourself they can always rejoin if they want to, and toss them overboard.

Dump the extra weight, keep your list lean and

engaged, and it will continue to perform for you even as it gets bigger and bigger. And that is, after all, the whole point.

Then off you go into the sunset, with a list of subscribers who hang on your every email, buy all your books, and will eventually rocket you to superstardom, because you are a Newsletter Ninja.

Afterword

Thanks so much for buying this book! I hope that it was helpful to you, and that you picked up at least a few tidbits that will improve your newsletter skills (or maybe more than a few).

I've tried to make it as comprehensive as I could; I definitely did not want to be one of those people whose book was really just a not-so-thinly-veiled advertisement for a course. I didn't want to hold back information in the hopes of increasing course signups, so I've tried to put everything I know into the book itself, trusting that if you need further help you will either seek me out or experiment on your own to find the best practices for your particular list.

I do teach a course, and you can read more about that in the next section, if you like (or skip it entirely), but here is my promise to you: Simply by reading this book and putting the techniques into practice, you *will* build a more engaged list, or re-engage the one you've got. I've also included some links in the Helpful Links section that showcase authors who are really doing their newsletters right. Because doing this stuff right means increased deliverability, better visibility, higher ranks, more earnings, and a steady influx of devoted mailing list subscribers who will help you get to the next level, and then the next.

I'll see you there!

Do You Need More Help? (aka The Inevitable Upsell)

I have further help available if this book wasn't quite enough to get you where you need to go. I don't imagine that comes as a surprise, so I'll keep this short and simple:

Several times a year, I teach a month-long course on all the topics I've covered here. The course includes help with creating subscriber avatars, list planning and setup, autoresponders, and deliverability and engagement. Each student has access to a weekly live lecture, and a thirty minute consult each week to help them implement the strategies in the way that's most effective for their situation. You can find information on the next available class by going to http://www.newsletterninja.net. Use the coupon code NN-2018 any time until the end of 2018, and get a 10% discount on your registration. (Please don't share that coupon code.)

I also do individual consulting on all aspects of mailing list creation and maintenance, as well as planning and writing autoresponders for authors who would rather contract that part of the process out. Email me at tammi@newsletterninja.net to inquire about prices and availability.

But, as I said before, I sincerely hope you've gotten enough out of this book that you don't need any further services from me—in which case, go do your thing. I'll be cheering you on from the sidelines as you finally conquer your newsletter issues.

Feel free to drop me a line and let me know how it's going!

Helpful Links

Rather than provide a bunch of links in a print book, because obviously you can't click on them and who the heck wants to type them out, I've put all the links up on their own page at the Newsletter Ninja website. Just visit newsletterninja.net/links!

Printed in Great Britain
by Amazon